Here's what others are saying about...

Leaving the City...

"Jeanie Peck has created an easy-to-read, thought-provoking guide for anyone thinking about moving to the country. Packed with timely tips on everything from planning the move to settling in, she's covered all the bases. Sprinkled with lessons she had to learn the hard way, this book gives readers a good overview of things to consider when getting ready to take the plunge into country life."

-Sandy Benson
Rural Property Bulletin

"Jeanie's book simultaneously entertains and educates you with her firsthand account of the trials and tribulations of her move. After reading her book, I would certainly recommend keeping it right by your side as you make your way from the city into the country."

-Lisa Linn Manley
SunDog LTD Reviews

On The Farm Press books are available at special quantity discounts for bulk purchases, for sales promotions, premiums, fund raising or educational use. Special books or book excerpts can also be created to fit specific needs.

For details write or email the office at:
On The Farm Press, Special Markets Dept.
PO Box 10445, Yakima, WA 98909
Email: info@OnTheFarmPress.com

Leaving the City

Jeanie Peck

On The Farm Press

On The Farm Press
PO Box 10445
Yakima, WA 98909
Email: info@OnTheFarmPress.com

Cover Design: Robert Howard
Art Work: Amorette Peck
Helping Editor: Dan Barge

Printed in the United States of America

ISBN# 0-9716174-2-2
Library of Congress Number: 2003115893

Table of Contents

Part IV: Making Money on the Homestead

Introduction

Deciding to move from the big city to a small town takes a lot of guts. There are many, many decisions to be made. If done properly and with care you can be one of the lucky folks who live in the country. Country living isn't for everyone. Many try to make the move but end up back in the city a few years later stating that they couldn't make the adjustments because it was too hard. Within this book I will give you the tools necessary to make awesome decisions and see if the country is where you wish to land!

A Good Old Country Boy explains it best when he says, "Even as you approach the city on its main freeway or express way, cars begin crowding closer together and dart in and out of lanes in an effort to get one or two car lengths ahead of the competitor. In the Country there is no such competition. Once on foot, the population of the city seems staggering to a small town person. It reminds you of an ant colony, or a cage with too many rats."

Please write to me if this book works for you, helps you or you just want to say hello and share a story with me. I love to receive mail!

Happy Property Hunting, Jeanie Peck

PO Box 10445, Yakima, WA 98909
info@OnTheFarmPress.com

Acknowledgments

Thank you: Sandy Benson from Rural Property Bulletin, Vicki Dunaway from Home Dairy News, author David Larkin from Houghton Mifflin Company for permissions taken from *Country Wisdom*, Marilyn Ross & Bob Bone for permissions taken from *Discover the Good Life in Rural America*.

And a special thanks to Dan Barge who helped me edit and edit and edit again. I couldn't have done this without you!

Other Books and Videos by the Author

Farm Animals: Your Guide to Raising Livestock
Video: Farrow to Finish (30 minutes)
Pigs and other stories
Leaving the City: 101 Tips for Moving to the Country

Newsletter
On The Farm Newsletter
12-16 pages, $12 year, $3 sample issue

Contact On The Farm Press to make a purchase, or see the order form in the back of this book!

Dedication

This book is dedicated to my three daughters, Shana who is the pumpkin in my garden, Amorette who is the silhouette in my night, and Kyra Jean who is the baby duck of my world.

Roses are Red
Violets are Green
It's a new beginning
Shana, Amo and Kyra Jean!

I love all three of you much,
Mama (Jeanie)

Warning - Disclaimer

This book is designed to provide information about the subject matter covered. It is sold with the understanding that the publisher and authors are not engaged in rendering legal, accounting or other professional services. If legal or other expert assistance is required, the services of a competent professional should be sought.

It is not the purpose of this manual to reprint all the information that is available, but to complement, amplify and supplement other texts. For more information, see the many references in the Resources.

Moving to the country or raising animals is not a get-rich scheme. Anyone who decides to move to the country or raise animals must expect to invest a lot of time and effort without any guarantee of success.

Every effort has been made to make this book as complete and accurate as possible. However, there may be mistakes both typographical and in content. Therefore, this text should be used only as a general guide and not as the ultimate source of moving or raising animals.

The purpose of this book is to educate and entertain. The author and On The Farm Press shall have neither liability nor responsibility to any person or entity with respect to any loss or damage caused or alleged to be caused directly or indirectly by the information contained in this book.

If you do not wish to be bound by the above, you may return this book to the publisher for a full refund.

Part I:
Planning; Before the Move

"Such gardens are not
made by singing: -- "Oh, how beautiful!"
and sitting in the shade."

-Rudyard Kipling, 1911

Why do you want to Move to the Country?

Are you looking for a change in your living habits? Want to make a clean change, get fresh air, take a walk with lots of room to wander around, visit with friendly neighbors and have a stress-free living opportunity?

I am here to let you know that the above changes will not resolve all of your current problems. It is possible to obtain a carefree, new and healthy lifestyle. But you have to work at it.

If you are thinking that a rural life will save you from the big-bad city life, think again. Folks that move from the city to the country just to escape the bad things that happened to them in the city don't usually last very long in the country.

Moving to the country changes your entire life. Take some time to decide why you want to move to the country. What do you want the country to do for you? What are your goals? Which habits will you need to change to make that happen? What tasks do you need to accomplish to make the change and the move?

As long as you realize that moving to the country isn't going to be a page out of a Martha Stewart magazine you have a chance of surviving the move. I know most of you don't have that sort of fairytale outlook on life, but those of you who do need to research country life more openly and decide if it is really what you want.

You can make a list of tasks and then cross each one off as you finish it. As you cross off more and more tasks, soon your goals will shape up into reality and you will be closer to your rural relocation every day. Moving to the country takes planning. There are many things you can do to make the move easily and as effortless as possible; for you and for your family members who move with you.

How we Moved to the Country and Survived

It isn't always easy or set in stone that you will survive the move to the country. Just because you want to do it doesn't make the move right for you. Some folks move to the country with the distinct picture in their minds that they will be riding an awesome stallion through the meadows wearing the perfect country clothing and a pretty cowboy hat. That isn't quite the way reality works.

As an example of what can happen, I am going to tell you our tale. Maybe by sharing our ups and downs with you now, I can spare you some of the hardships we incurred. Then I give you the 101 tips to use wisely before making your own move to the country. Enjoy!

Moving usually takes planning. Lots of it. It's amazing how caught up in the moment folks can get when they are planning big events. It's not just the packing that needs to be planned out. Think about every aspect of what you want out of the move and the relocation.

After spending weekends in Okanogan County over the prior year, Ron and I decided we wanted to move there. It is beautiful, green, there are trees and it doesn't rain every day. I had two daughters from a previous relationship and Ron and I wanted to give them a healthy, happy and safer life than we could offer them in the suburb of Seattle which we then lived.

One evening while we sat in the hot tub talking and sharing dreams, we joked about flipping a coin to decide our fate. Heads we would move to Okanogan County and start a new life together. Tails we would wait until it was all planned out and we could sell our house first. The coin landed on heads.

We put the house in Auburn up for sale the next day and it sold the following week to the first guy who came to see it. It was sure scary to sell your own home before you bought or looked at another to buy. I don't recommend doing this!

I couldn't go with Ron to find our home in Okanogan. I had to finish up my two weeks at work and start all the packing. It didn't matter what the house looked like anyway. I was ready to make the jump.

What I didn't plan for was the climate, which included major snow fall, neighbors, the longer drive to the nearest town and the fact that I didn't have any special skills to get a job in a small town. I suggest you look at each of these items closely before you decide to move to a small town. Once all of your ducks are in a row then continue on with the journey.

Okanogan County is beautiful! I encourage you to visit there even today just to see what I am talking about. But you must plan for it if you intend to move there. We didn't. We hadn't given in to the temptation to give up and move back to the city either. Here is what we did do.

Ron and Shana (my oldest daughter) drove down to Okanogan and started house hunting. I gave my two weeks notice at my current job in the city and started packing up the house. We had already sold the house remember, so we had to move within sixty days and let the new owner move in. Ron and Shana found a nice three bedroom mobile home on five acres in the outskirts of Okanogan and we moved into the house thirty days later.

When buying property, I'm sure it goes without saying that you should meet any direct neighbors and make sure they are compatible to live close by you. We didn't do this. Coming from the city, we felt that having only one neighbor was the ticket to paradise. Our only neighbor was about 600 feet away. In the city we had lived about three feet from the next door neighbor. 600 feet seemed like a lifetime away until the trouble began.

Okanogan took us by surprise the first winter. The snow started falling and a major first time in twenty year blizzard began and didn't stop until we had four feet of ice and snow covering our driveway and yard. It made it impossible to leave the property. That snow also forced us to invest in a 1965 Ford Tractor for $6000. It became one of the best unsuspected buys we made over the next few years. That was 1995.

I didn't have any special working skills so I took a home class to learn the skill of medical transcription. I finished in nine months (early for the two year course) and took a job in Omak with a medical clinic. I loved the job and worked there the next two years.

At home things were piling up around us. It was spring and I wanted a garden. We shared a water well with the neighbor. They made it perfectly clear that we didn't have irrigation rights. I wasn't going to have a garden! We finally came to a compromise and paid them for the water every month.

But each time we tried something different that included water, the neighbors were hanging over our shoulders or fence to see what it entailed. Once the sprinkler ran two feet into a small pen that held our baby emu birds. I didn't even know it. I had the sprinkler watering our lawn next to the pen and when the pressure built up the sprinkler began to water the birds pen as well. It took about ten minutes before the neighbor was over complaining that we didn't have irrigation rights so what are we trying to pull? Did we think they couldn't see us watering those birds from just down the road?

In 1996 Ron and I married in the comfort of our own country yard setting. All of our family and friends came. It was a special event. I became pregnant and by October 1997 our little Kyra Jean arrived.

During this time I bought a dog since I was home alone a lot. To help out the community I bought from the local dog pound. Elvis was the sweetest black lab you could ever hope for. He was gentle even though his tail could clean all the pretty stuff off any table he passed by within a split second. It was a powerful tail!

After two years of arguing back and forth with the neighbor over the shared well, a lot of small things that I can't remember and our dog (they didn't want us to have a dog even though he only barked when he had a reason and he stayed in our yard), Elvis, came up missing one morning. We found out many days later that the neighbor shot and killed our dog.

Now we had three beautiful daughters, a dog the neighbors killed, a fight with the same neighbors over the water rights to use their well, and finally they hired a lawyer to try and make *us* pay to install their new well.

This is when I put my foot down and said, "lets move away from these quacks and make a new start." And Ron agreed since the whole water issue had went through a lawyer and cost us a pretty penny before we won the case. It could never be pleasant living next door to them after that much hassle.

When house hunting, I suggest going to neighbors' houses and asking questions that will give you a good idea of what sort of folks they are before moving in to a house. It seems trivial but you just never know what sort of neighbors you'll have unless you check them out first. It could save you years of agony.

We found a rural 40 acre setting which we thought was perfect because the closest neighbor was a miles walk away from our home. Our home was a 45 minute drive one-way to the closest town, which was Tonasket, Washington.

The first year on the mountain we found out that the winters never seem to end. We still had our trusty 1965 tractor and I don't think we would have survived without it. We did have to buy a quality plow for winter.

Ron was working out of town and had to drive home on the weekends to be with us. His drive was three hours and forty minutes one-way. Ron drove home on Thursday nights and returned to work on Sundays. The drive was very taxing on him. (And I'm sure this is one of the reasons we didn't make it as a team. We grew apart with too much time alone).

Just a small recommendation: Country life takes two people to make it work; unless you start out alone. If you move in together and share the work load, remember that if one of you are called away for work or other things for a long period of time, all that work on the farm will be dumped on the person left behind. Make sure this is what you both agree on. I would suggest finding an area to live in that both of you can come home every night and work on your dreams and goals together.

Meanwhile I was adjusting to the newness of rural life. The kids' school bus stop was a twenty minute drive every morning and every afternoon. It was hard to plan your day when it was broken up like that. If I needed to go to town I had to plan very carefully to be back in time to pick the girls up.

The road we lived on didn't offer a school bus at the end of our driveway. There just weren't enough children on the rural road to make it worthwhile for the county. You should make sure you are willing to go the extra mile before committing yourself to such exhausting daily schedules.

There were other things we all had to adjust to as well. Such as the fact that we only had wood heat. No central floor heat was available in this house. Ron and I had to make sure there was enough wood stacked up outside to get us through the winter;  which lasted all the way until the end of May! Even in August we got a hail storm and it froze a lot of my garden vegetables.

By summertime I started buying animals by the dozens. Baby animals of course. I love the babies. We didn't have any pens built so Ron was upset about that. He had to spend a few weekends getting us all set up for the animals. In the meantime the rest of us spent those weeks catching and re-penning escaped pigs, goats and calves.

So, of course I suggest that you get your pens ready for each animal *before* you buy them. It's only fair to the animals and the builder of the pens.

I set up a garden but since we didn't check out the climate before moving here (we just wanted to get away from the previous neighbors), I wasn't aware that I would never, ever be able to plant corn, melons, tomatoes, green peppers or cucumbers. And I like to can food for winter eating.

It would be a good idea to check out the local climate of your proposed property and be sure you will be able to do what you want with the place.

The second year our 14 foot hand dug well went dry. This was one of the most taxing events we shared on the mountain. We called the well digger and he was extremely busy that year. Our name was added to his list and we kept in touch.

Meanwhile the kids and I had to go to town and bum water from my mom's. She didn't mind. But I had to take the kids there to shower, (it was a forty five minute drive to get there) sometimes before school in the morning, sometimes in the evening. Mom let us fill all of our gallon milk cartons with water so we could fill the toilet tank at home and be able to flush the toilet. We also filled five gallon containers for drinking, cooking and teeth brushing water. I never had such hassles in my entire life.

Another situation was the amount of water that horses or cows drink in one day. Up to 14 gallons each. Ron had to fill barrels of water for this chore on the weekends and make sure we had enough to last through the week while he was gone. Very time consuming when on a farm there are so many things to do.

Without water, the laundry piled up. Mom didn't have a washer and dryer so we had to go to town to do laundry. It usually cost about $25.00 to do ten loads. And it was not a nice experience after owning a washer and dryer for so long.

Picture this: Your switching your clothes from the washer to the dryer and the creep at the end of the row with warn out clothes and gaps between his teeth won't look the other way. You are watching his penetrating eyes to be safe about what he might be thinking and you drop your sexiest panties on the floor in front of the dryer. You know the mistake was made as soon as his eyes drop to take a peak and they glaze over in happiness!

Anyway, after waiting so long and hearing from other folks about well diggers making lots of profit by digging up holes all over your property because they can't actually detect where the water will be when they start, we called a witcher for advice.

Ron found a witcher, which is a person who waves a wand around and can tell you exactly where the water will be under the ground and how much water you should get from that source. We paid $500 and they guaranteed that their guess would be within 10 feet of the proposed plan.

This witcher was right on the money. I suggest that you use a witcher to save you money and time and of course the headaches that go with not getting what you paid for. But remember, check them out and it helps if they guarantee their work. That would show you that they are respectable.

Finally the new well was in and we had water. See my notes later in Part II about what to look for and who to hire before paying any money to a well digger. We learned a lot from this experience and I am passing the tips on to you!

Living on the mountain was hard on all of us. I finally switched the two older kids to home schooling and they did most of their work from a computer in their rooms. The smallest one wasn't old enough for school. Home schooling takes a lot of time and effort on the parents part but I feel the just rewards are well worth the headaches of learning a new way of doing things.

Five years in that house took its toll on the husband and myself. We grew apart since he worked away from home during the week and couldn't concentrate on us as a couple during the weekends. There was much work to do on the weekend and we didn't get the needed time alone as a couple.

We went our separate ways after eight years and sold the farm. Now I am planning a move to the country to start over with the kids and this is where I hope these pieces of paper will become an asset for you. Since I started writing this book before the separation, you will hear me talk about us in a present tone of voice, and in a past tone, I hope that isn't too confusing.

This book does not go into depth about one subject we discuss. Rather, it is to introduce the options to you so you can get an educated guess and decide which route will be best for you to proceed. There are a number of useful resources in the back of the book so you can learn more about the subjects that interest you most.

Of course deciding to move to the country can be a strenuous act in itself. Below are a few ideas to keep in mind to help you make your decisions more wisely. You don't want to move to your dream land to find that it is really a nightmare. Before deciding to make the move to the country, please try a few of these suggestions to see if living in the country will work for you and your family. It is not for everyone.

There are many small tasks you can complete before you even look at property to buy in the country.

Taking the time to prepare for rural life can make all the difference in the world. Before quitting your high paid job in the city, read the first part of this book and put the suggestions to use. If you can accomplish these tasks before you buy property, you might have a better chance of making it where other city folks have failed. Good luck and remember to write and share your stories with me.

Include Kids in the Move

It probably goes without saying that you need to include the kids as much as possible in a relocation. Kids can be devastated by losing their friends, their place in the community, their status at school, etc.

Even though we tend to think, 'kids bounce back easily', it's a good idea to try and make the adjustment as effortless as possible for them.

Sometimes the difference between a happy kid and an unhappy one is the simple difference between the involvement the parents gave them in family decision making.

If the kids are included in the major family decisions, and it would be up to each parent to decide what would be major decisions to include them in, then the kids will also learn how to make choices when they are older.

Getting Kids Involved in the Country

The earliest age you can get your children opting for the same adventures in country living as you have, the better!

Kids can be a great help on the farm or in the country. They can collect eggs, mow the lawn, pull weeds, help in the garden, pick up unwanted rocks, etc.

 If you wait until the kids are teen-agers then you might lose their interests in a country adventure. By this age they are into TV and school classmates and video games and they won't think helping you out is going to be fun or adventurous! You need to start them at the earliest possible age to retain their interests.

Stop Buying Stuff you Don't Need

What do I mean? Each and every time you decide to buy something stop and ask yourself a few questions:

♥ Do I really need this item?
♥ Is this essential to my health?
♥ Will I miss this if I don't buy it now?
♥ Can I live without this?

If you can, make a list of the things you wish to buy and keep the highest priorities at the top of the list. If you still have to have them in two weeks then maybe you should buy them. But if you can't remember why you needed them so bad then you just saved some money! Put it in the bank.

Between TV commercials and magazines the city makes you feel as if you need to buy things that you really don't need. You know the things I am talking about. Just look in your closets and garage and you'll remember. Ask the above questions before you buy anything and you'll start saving money sooner.

According to figures published by the National Association of Realtors, an average family of four in Los Angeles would spend 30% more than one in Rangely, Colorado to achieve the same life-style.

> "If Eden be on Earth at all, 'Tis that which we the country call."
>
> -Henry Vaughan

Pay Off Credit Card Debt

I highly recommend you try living within a smaller budget while you have a higher income before jumping into the rural life-style. Make sure you can handle the change. Here's one thing I suggest as a test. Start paying double or even triple on your credit card debts. Pay them off as soon as you can.

Don't buy something unless you can pay cash for it. Keep the cards in a drawer for emergencies but don't use them unless a *true emergency* arises. You do have to be disciplined for this situation to work.

What will this do for you? It will get you out of debt so that you can move to the country without a huge debt load on your shoulders. It is easier to live within your means if you start fresh without monthly debt (not including a mortgage).

The reason I don't suggest you toss those credit cards into the garbage is because you can use the cards as emergency fund money in case you lose your job or have a family crisis before you have had time to save up your emergency fund.

Buy Older Vehicles

Save enough cash so you can buy a used vehicle. Once you have the money saved and the used car picked out and bought, *then* it is time to sell any vehicles you pay a monthly debt to keep. Not only will your monthly auto insurance costs go down, but you will also be able to put the money saved from usual car payments into savings and start your emergency fund.

The reason I suggest you do this is because once you move to the country it is not as easy to come up with monthly payments for debts owed. You will live further from a city and possibly be living on half the income you now survive on.

Any debts you can sell or pay off before moving to the country will give you an advantage when you start looking for property to buy. The money you save can either go into savings or go towards an emergency fund.

Living Expenses for Emergencies

Start a savings account and put any extra money you save into it. Did you sell your auto yet and buy a used car? If you did, you can put that monthly payment into savings! Or if you sold the vehicle and made a profit; put that into savings!

Stop buying more than you need. Put the extra money aside and you'll notice a large sum of money that you usually waste start building a real nice savings account.

Once you have about eight months worth of usual monthly living expenses saved, you have an excellent emergency fund for your family in the event that you lose your job.

Suze Orman explains in her book *The 9 Steps to Financial Freedom* that you do have to decide what the usual living expenses are before you will know what amount is needed to save for this emergency fund.

The dollar amounts to add up are the things you buy on a monthly basis to live. *Not* the extra things you buy because they are pretty. Those are extras. Ask yourself before every purchase you make, "Do I really *need* this?"

You have to add up the food costs, auto fuel, electric bill, phone bill, mortgage, auto insurance, property taxes, etc. The actual costs of living.

Other expenses will cease or be cut way back after moving to the country. If you sold your vehicle then you are already saving between $200-$400 a month. This was an extra debt. You should now *own* your car, saving the above amount every month all year long!

Once you have a monthly expense total, multiply that by eight and you have the amount that should be in your emergency fund. Yes, it could take a year or more to save this fund but once it is there if you should lose your job or have a family emergency you will have the funds to take care of monthly expenses without going further into debt. If you are reputitious about saving then the funds will grow faster than you can imagine.

Advanced First-Aid Class

It is advisable to have your entire family take an advanced
class in first aid. If you live in
the country you might not have
time to wait for an ambulance
to come to you. Take the initia-
tive now and prepare your family for emergencies later.

Living on the mountain I was always worried that if
something were to happen how on earth would I get
my family member (if they were seriously hurt) to the
hospital in time when it took 45 minutes to drive there.

Just think if someone lost a body limb and had to be
rushed to the hospital, with a 45 minute drive, they
would probably bleed to death before I could get them
there if I didn't know how to cinch off the body parts to
stall the bleeding on the drive to the hospital. We
learned that in a first-aid class!

Survival Kit

Sit down with your family and see what different needs
each person has. Does one child need a bee kit for
allergies? Does another need motion sickness pills on
hand for traveling? Make a list of each person's needs
and get these things together for your survival kit.

Next get together things that will help you in emergencies on the road. Here I list the basics but it's up to you to decide what your family needs in your survival kit. Each kit can be different. In case you get stranded on the side of the road you might want to put in your kit:

Flashlight w/extra Batteries
Warm Blanket(s)
First Aid Kit
Hat & Gloves
Boots & Extra Socks
Gallon of Water
Jumper Cables
Fire Extinguisher
Snacks that won't mold
Canned Foods w/opener
Medicines for Family
Socket/Wrench Set
Screw Driver Set
Electrical Tape/Duct Tape
Toilet Paper/Hand Towels

Remember that it depends on what type of climate you live in and the time of year plays a role in deciding what to include in your survival kit.

Consider Medical and Emergency

Do you need to be close to dental or medical services? Keep this in mind when you choose a permanent home site. And use the phone book to make sure the health care needs that you have are offered in that area.

No one in our immediate family has a medial concern (other than bee sting allergies) that we should be closer to medical services for. Thank goodness. For us, if someone gets hurt we need the ambulance to come 45 minutes out of town to our home in the mountains. So, we try to be careful up here and we know the basics of how to care for simple wounds.

Don't find a home too far from medical services if you suspect you will have a need for those services often. Such as for diabetes, heart disease, cancer treatments, etc. You get the idea.

Elderly Care Facilities

Remember to check the area for elderly care facilities if you will require those services in the future.

Building Basics

Learn the basics of building, squaring up buildings and any other things you can learn before moving to the country. See if you can volunteer with a crew of construction workers to get your skills up to par before trying to build your own sheds, etc.

Learn Electric Tricks of the Trade

Just like above, see if you can volunteer with an electrician for a day or two to get the basics of the art down. In the country it is likely more difficult to get an electrician to come to your home if you live too far out of the city. Sometimes it will be more useful for you to do your own simple jobs. And less costly.

Take Special Classes

It would be optimal if you were able to work from your home in the country. You never know the number of miles to the nearest town or city until you move there. There could be a long commute between you and your work place. If you are able to work from any where you sit, all the better. Keep this in mind.

If you need to, take the classes while you are still living in the city. The computer is your friend. But there are lots of work abilities you can learn to do. I will cover a lot of other areas you can conquer to make income on the farm in Part IV of this book.

"There is one thing about hens that looks like wisdom --they don't cackle much till they have laid their eggs."

-Josh Billings, 1878

Right now I would suggest looking into a trade class for medical transcription, medical assistant, veterinarian assistant, hair dresser, computer skills so you can fix computers for folks, typing skills, auto repair, etc.

Buy Tools at Garage Sales

Think about what you will be doing in the country and watch for sales at local garage sales. You can pick up things like a good quality (and don't buy cheap crap here, you need your tools to stand up to the dirt in the country) shovel, pick, wheelbarrow, hammer, small garden tools, a rake and a good set of tools for car use.

Also a come-along rachet hoist (winch), chain saw, carpenters square, circular saw, handsaw, chisels of various sizes, etc.

The biggest expense that I would suggest would be a good quality generator. With this investment, you can supply your family with electricity during power outages and such. Just because you want to live in the country doesn't mean you need to do without the necessities in life. Be comfortable and keep your family smiling by covering all your basics. See "Generator'.

Books on Building

Collect at sales (when looking for tools) the books you will need to educate yourself about things you will want to do for yourself when you live in the country.

We have a library of books on the animals we like to raise, buildings we need or want to build ourselves and fences we will need to build as well. It is important to learn about squaring up buildings so the rest of the project goes smoothly. I could never get that part figured out but luckily the man knows what to do in my family.

 Think about what you want to do in the country. Do you want to start bee keeping and give away honey to family and friends at Christmas time?

Want to raise a pig, cow, sheep or goat for your freezer needs? How about chickens to collect your own fresh eggs and sell extras to friends? What about rabbits? Of course I would recommend my first book *Farm Animals; Your Guide to Raising Livestock* as a starter point for raising any of the above animals.

Or small purebred dogs for extra income? Whatever your desire, read, buy or collect every book on the subject. It is my suggestion to first borrow the books from the library then buy the best ones to reference later.

Get Used to 'Slowing Down'

Everything moves slower in the country. People are not in a hurry to get anywhere. Believe me, it takes awhile to get used to this. In the city you pass the slow drivers but in the country you need to be patient. There might only be a one lane road for miles and miles and it may not be safe to pass.

Try getting used to this idea while you are still in the city. Make sure you give yourself enough time to get to places without the worry of driving fast. Leave earlier.

"A road like this was not built for anyone in a hurry. It follows every curve of the stream ...approaches the covered bridge at a right angle... turns abruptly and disappears into the dark mouth of the tunnel."
-Helen Hooven Santmyer

TV

Do you really need a television? I truly feel that families stuck together and worked hard to be helpful back in the olden days before the television was invented. If you can't get rid of the television all together, why not set up times when it's okay to watch it?

When the kids get home from school, they should be doing their homework and then some chores to give them the character and tools they will need to learn in order to take charge of their own lives when they move out.

If you let the television be your baby-sitter then you can't blame anyone but yourself when your kid acts out from what they learn on the tube.

Why not take the time on weekends and teach the teenagers to cook a few different simple meals so they can do some of the cooking during the week days?

Not only does this take a load off your back after working hard all day long but it gives the kids the cooking skills they need to learn before they move out.

In the country there are so many, many things to do instead of watching television. Yes, we own a television set but we don't have cable TV or any stations. We choose when the television is turned on by renting movies when we decide the work load is light enough on the farm.

Offer Services in Return For Theirs

Get to know your neighbors. Let them know what you do for a living or on the side. And if they have a service to offer you, remember that you can barter here.

When you move to the country you might need someone's tractor to plow your garden spot. Maybe you know how to do something for them and can trade services for the use of their tractor. Both of you get your projects completed and there is no need to exchange money.

This is another reason it would benefit you to introduce yourself to your new neighbors before moving in. See what they do for a living and how it can benefit you in the future.

> "The arrival of anybody was the cause for what my mother always called 'putting on the big pot and the little pot, too."
>
> -Celestine Sibley

Get the Family Involved

I touch on this subject later in the 'Family and Friends' section but I will get a note of it mentioned here as well. If you have family members that can be of benefit to you in a country atmosphere, try and get them involved! Tell them what your plans are for the country and if they are interested see what they have to offer.

 Maybe you know an aunt that can sew blankets to sell at the markets, or can jams and veggies to sell to neighbors. Or a grown up daughter who wants to invest in your farm or country adventure in one way or another. How do you know what is offered unless you ask and then seek their interest?

> "If a person is industrious, and so fortunate as to have a family capable of joining in his labors, and living in the bonds of affection, there can be no doubt that he will prosper."
>
> -James Pickering, 1832

Buy in Bulk

Another great thing to get used to while still in the city is to buy food and household products in bulk. I go to Costco. I find they have most of what I need to stock the pantry for the year. I usually do this in the fall.

Just take note of the personal hygiene products your family uses. Deodorant, toothpaste, vitamins, shampoo and conditioner, body soap, hand soap, dish soap, laundry soap, napkins, paper towels and toilet paper.

Now try to decide how much of each item each person in the family uses; like for us we use eight packages of toothpaste. I buy eight to last us the year.

Do this for each product your family needs. Yes, it costs more but you save time and money buying in bulk and making one stop at Costco rather than a lot of stops all year long to the grocery stores.

Do the same thing for food that is easily stored in bulk. Like soups, coffee and creamer, flour, sugar, tea, soda pop, juice, noodles, rice, etc.

And if you have a freezer it is nice to store butter, hamburger, sausage, bacon, pork products you like and any other meats that freeze well and you can buy in bulk to save money. You can even check with your local meat processor for these needs.

Another nice thing buying in bulk does for you is it saves you the time of the weekly shopping chores. Now you have most of what you need right at your finger tips. If you come home tired and just don't want to cook a big meal, chances are you can put together something simple right from your pantry and freezer!

Cook in Bulk

If you are buying in bulk you mine as well cook in bulk, too. I cook for three days and relax for three months. Since this would need a lot of explaining and I don't have the time to go into it in detail here, I am going to suggest you get a copy of *Jeanie's Awesome Big Cook Booklet* which has enough information and recipes to supply you with 40+ dinners in the freezer. See my website at http://www.OnTheFarmPress.com

Here is one of my Big Cook Day recipes to get you started and see if you like the idea of relaxing and visiting in the living room with your family while the dinner cooks in the kitchen each night!

Recipe: Stroganoff

- ♥ 4 pounds hamburger
- ♥ 3 medium onions
- ♥ 4 cans cream of mushroom soup
- ♥ 4 cups of milk
- ♥ 1 teaspoon paprika
- ♥ 2 teaspoons pepper
- ♥ 32 oz sour cream
- ♥ 32 oz wide egg noodles (bought the day the dinner is thawed -or use toast)

1. Brown meat and onion; drain.
2. Stir in soup, milk and paprika.
3. Cover and simmer 15 minutes.
4. Stir in sour cream and heat but don't boil.
5. Cook noodles and drain or prepare toast.
6. Serve over noodles or hot toast.

Makes 8 dinners for a family of five. With this recipe you can store the sauce for the dinner in the freezer until you are ready to use it; and make the noodles or toast the night of the dinner.

Garden in Containers

While still living in the city you can plant tomatoes and cucumbers on your patio if you don't have a piece of ground to dig up. Practice with tomatoes or green and red peppers.

One of the ideas that city folks have about gardening is that you need a large yard or some acreage to achieve your garden growing goals. Not true. In *Backyard Market Gardening*, Andy Lee makes a point that a back yard is an excellent first farm. Nothing is too small.

Use those old three-five gallon laundry soap buckets. Just wash them out real good, pop a few holes in the bottom for drainage and fill with good dirt.

What I do is get a few rocks for the very bottom of the container to encourage good drainage, then add some dirt from the yard for the bottom half of the container, and fill the top half with the best soil I can find.

Consideration for Your Dogs

Before you find that perfect spot of property you should consider the following when preparing your pets for the country:

♥ If you are moving out of state you will need to find out what the border regulations are for up to date vaccinations for your dogs.

♥ Try to keep to the same routines, such as meal times, walks and eating, so the dog doesn't get stressed out.

♥ Bring your dogs favorite bed, toy and bowls for comfort to your pet during the drive.

♥ While you are packing up the house and truck, keep your dog in a kennel until you are finished. Dogs will get very distressed if they feel some thing is going on and they don't understand what it is you are doing.

The fun doesn't stop once you move into your new home either. You still need to watch your animal for signs of distress. After you move into your new country home:

♥ Keep dogs on a chain until they know where they are and where they belong.

♥ Let them learn about the environment around you before setting them free out in the country.

♥ Teach them about electric fences or shock collars if you plan to use those.

Check into Daycare

There are times when you might need daycare in the country. If both parents work then you will need to be sure this service is covered. Take a day and check out what is offered in the new location.

Two Income Families

It needs to be mentioned somewhere that two income families will have repercussions in the household if one income is deleted when moving to the country. This is something you both need to discuss before making the decision to move.

Granted, living in the country may cost you considerably less than living in the city, but not if you still have all the same bills you carried when living in the city. That is why I took the time in this chapter to prepare you and ask you to prepare yourself for a lesser income.

Go back to the first part of this chapter and read all the recommendations that I ask of you and take care of those needs before moving to the country. I can't stress enough: *the less you carry on your shoulders when you move, the easier and better adjusted you will be when you arrive in the country.*

Special Needs for Children

There are times when a family has a child with special needs. Take this into consideration before moving that child away from everything they have ever known. Make sure it won't devastate that child into submission and depression.

If you will be relocating the child to a new school, take the time to meet with new teachers to evaluate any special needs the child will have in the new school. Be sure the new school has those services available.

Home Schooling Test for Your Kids

I have been amazed at what I've heard from other parents who don't know much about home schooling. They think it is set up for children who are trouble makers. Not true. They ask me "how do your kids learn their social skills?"

I have to sit down and tell them a few things I learned while researching the idea of home schooling my kids.

Then I tell them about a few tests I did and what I learned from those tests. And I ask them one simple question; to define social skills.

Social skills can mean different things to different people. To me it is the basis to every child's learning ability. They learn this at home long before we send them off to kindergarten.

> "School-days, school-days, dear old golden rule days, readin' and ritin' and 'rithmetic, taught to the tune of a hick'ry stick."
> -Will D. Cobb

In my eyes, social skills are equal to being able to converse with other adults and children alike, talking in public or in front of a room full of people, having proper etiquette when on the phone, giving respect to adults even if they are strangers, and more.

Some parents answered that they felt their kids learned social skills in public schools; where else would they learn about life? I couldn't keep my mouth closed (I rarely can when I believe in something) when they told me this. I told them to perform a test when they went home that evening.

Here's the test you can perform on any teenager that has been in public school. If you know of a home schooled teenager try it on them next and measure the differences. You be the judge.

Just ask the teenager to make a phone call to one of your adult friends. Ask your friend ahead of time to talk with them as if they were an adult... and see what happens. I bet they can't keep up and will say 'um' or ask 'what?' a lot.

My theory is that kids in public school are not taught to converse with adults. They learn all of their lives to talk to other kids their own ages. It's one of the reasons these kids get out on their own and fail in the first year. They're not taught some of the skills which are needed as adults.

School Comparison From 1940

Here is a comparison made from teachers of public schools in 1940. They did the same comparison 40 years later and those results are below as well.

1940: Teachers were asked what were the worst problems with children in class.

- ♥ Talking in class
- ♥ Chewing gum
- ♥ Tossing papers on the floor, not in the garbage can

1980: Teachers were asked what were the worst problems with children in class.

- Rape
- Vandalism
- Burglary
- Teenage pregnancy
- Drugs and alcohol
- Foul language

Teaching Your Own Child the Basics

I think we need to quit pawning off the job of teaching our children on the teachers. It's our job to do the basics. I realize every parent can't be home with their children in today's world; most families are broken and both parents need to work in order to survive. But what about when the work day ends and you are home all evening with your children?

What can you do? Well, why not get that growing child in the kitchen and teach them a few things about cooking? They need to learn more than making pancakes or an omelet; which is what they learn in home economics these days. Give them the skills they need to survive without you in this world!

What else? Why not start a project together to give them even more of a chance for success in the future?

You can start the project together and work on it in the evenings instead of sitting in front of a television like a bump on a log.

A few ideas would include sewing, crocheting, quilting a blanket, drawing, cross-stitch, arts and crafts, writing poems or keeping a journal or building something like a birdhouse in the garage, appliance repair, auto repair and computer programming.

What sort of skills do you want your child to know when they turn eighteen and move out on their own? Can you teach them what *you* do at work? A few ideas might include:

♥ Keep a curriculum schedule
♥ Hold a conversation with people of any age
♥ Fill out an application for employment
♥ Maintain a checkbook that doesn't bounce
♥ Cook, clean and basic auto maintenance
♥ What it means to run a household
♥ How to shop and get the best deals

> "A traveler, describing a very quiet village, said, 'It was... so still at night that I could almost hear my bed tick."
> -The Old Farmer's Almanac, 1878

Hope of a Healthier and Better Life

Moving to the country isn't for everyone. But we are all born with some ability to learn and adapt to new things. Decide what is best for you and go with that idea!

Joel Salatin author of *You Can Farm* states, "It doesn't matter what your background, your social-economic status, your age or your current living condition if you have a yearning in your soul to grow things and minister healthy food to people."

Joel also reminds us that, "If you are more concerned about what the neighbors will say when you convert your lawn into garden beds than you are about getting started in farming, you're too peer-dependent and would not do things differently enough to succeed even if you did have more acreage. Better to find this out now than later."

Some new homesteaders are quickly disillusioned after suffering hardships of the homestead life and they end up back in the city soon after. It is my hope that you will be one of those who make it work for you in the country!

Part II
As you Search

*"I see no virtues
where I smell no sweat"*

-Francis Quarles, 1640

Getting Started

I'm sure you remember a farm from your childhood and would love nothing more than to return to that memory. Great. Do you want a few acres or a 1000 acre ranch? Do you want to have the place ready for you to move in directly, or do you mind finishing up the place yourself? What region do you want to live in? What state?

After deciding on the above questions, then you need to decide whether to rent a house for awhile and scope out the area, or buy your house right away. I'd suggest renting in a small town for at least a year to see if you really like the area and surrounding opportunities. A big house for sale down the road could arise later and if you already bought your present home, you might miss the chance of a lifetime. On the other hand, if you know with all your heart that you could live in a particular house for the rest of your life, then go for it.

Be careful when buying country property if you have never lived on a farm or rural location before. There is a difference from living in a condominium in the city. Do your research. That said, here are a few things to ask and watch for when buying property in the country.

Rural, Country or Wilderness

What is the difference between rural, country and wilderness? Rural is when the post office doesn't have a mail box for you. Country is when you have to drive a distance to your home and everyone waves hello to you along the way. And Wilderness is when you drive for days and the helicopter still has to drop a box from the sky to get it in to your house by Christmas!

> Rural is from Old French, or from late Latin *ruralis*, from 'country'. In early use little difference exists between *rural* and *rustic*, but later usage shows rural in connection with locality and country scenes, with *rustic* being reserved for the primitive qualities of country life.

Okay, that sort of explains the differences between rural and country together -since they are pretty close to being the same these days, but what about the wilderness scene? Where does that come in to play?

> Wilderness is Old English *wildeornes* and was a 'land inhabited only by wild animals', based on *wild deor* 'wild deer' and the noun suffix *-ness*.

There you go! If you think you live rural, rustic or in the country you can tell your friends that, and if you live with bears and wild deer then you can tell them you live in the wilderness.

Searching for the Country Dream

Bob Bone, author of *Discover the Good life in Rural America* suggests you phone for a copy of United National Real Estate's $5.95 catalog, *United Country* at 800-999-1020.

Bob states that *United Country Catalog* features hundreds of rural real estate residences, ranches and businesses all over America and is the only national catalog of its type. United Country is published twice a year and contains a representative selection of real estate from each of United National's offices throughout the United States.

Bob also offers more information: When you call to buy your catalog tell the representative what kind of property you have in mind, the area of the country you are considering and your price range. United will relay the information to their affiliates nearest the area of your interest and they in turn will mail you their free regional 'Real Estate Previews'.

> Country Tip:
> You can buy more property than you need, section it off and sell one half to pay for your own half. Or buy a larger chunk of property, place your home in the middle and protect yourself from encroachment.

Rural Property Bulletin

Are you still looking for that perfect farm?

Magazine helps property seekers chase their dreams

Have you always dreamed of buying a 160-acre farm in Ohio? How about a 2,500-acre buffalo ranch in Kansas? Or a rustic fishing camp on a lake in Wisconsin? Maybe a cabin tucked into Montana's Bitterroot Mountains or North Carolina's mountain country would suit you better. How about a seaside cottage nestled in a quiet spot on the Oregon coast? If you've been dreaming of finding that ideal place in the country, here's a publication where you'll find all of these and hundreds more every month!

Since 1980 the folks at Rural Property Bulletin have been helping people find farms, ranches, retreats, recreation property, and homes in the country. Every month, subscribers enjoy a magazine packed with rural and small-town bargains for sale nationwide.

And yes, there are still some bargains out there. Recent listings have included $300 per acre pasture land in North Dakota, a $5,500 home in Minnesota, 18 acres with a 3 bedroom home in Arkansas for $59,000, 160 acres on a river in Ontario, Canada, for $14,284, a cabin on 5 acres with a view of Mt. McKinley, Alaska, for $55,000, an office building in a small Nebraska town for $9,500, 400 acres with a pond in Maine for $160,000, and a big country home on 40 Missouri acres for under $125,000. Many of the properties are offered with owner financing.

Looking for a way to make a living when you move to the country? RPB also has a section on rural and small town businesses for sale. You'll find quite a variety of them. In a recent issue opportunities included a horse shoeing business in Pennsylvania, a country inn on a lake in Wisconsin, a British Columbia (Canada) resort with cabins and campsites, and a mom & pop café in a small town in Texas.

Publisher Sandy Benson says, "Rural Property Bulletin is an ideal tool for people who are thinking of relocating to the countryside but haven't yet decided on a specific location. RPB gives them a chance to compare prices and offerings in different parts of the country."

Benson started Rural Property Bulletin back in 1980, when she had a piece of property in north Idaho that she was having a hard time selling. "I knew I would have to advertise out of the area to find a buyer, because the local economy was terribly depressed at the time," she said. "The closest big-city newspaper was in Seattle, and I tried an ad in that. It cost a couple hundred bucks, and I didn't get any response!"

That experience taught her that there was a need for a publication where private individuals with rural property for sale could advertise beyond their immediate locale, for a reasonable price.

Rural Property Bulletin began as an eight-page regional newsletter, covering properties for sale just in the pacific northwest. It didn't take long for requests to come in to expand to nationwide coverage. Today the Bulletin is a 52-page magazine featuring properties offered for sale by both owners and agents across the United States and Canada.

New subscribers looking to buy or sell property get a free 40-word classified ad (there's a "wanted" section too!)

A sampling of Rural Property Bulletin's ads can be viewed at their website, www.RuralProperty.net. Property seekers can order a one-year subscription for $28 (first class mail) or $16 (bulk mail.) A sample copy is $3.

To order, contact Sandy at Rural Property Bulletin, PO Box 369-F, Bassett, NE 68714 or call toll free 888-FARM-BUY (327-6289) with credit card information.

Chamber of Commerce

One thing you could do to learn more about the climate of a possible city or town you wish to live in is to ask for an information packet from the chamber of commerce there. This packet can tell you all you need to know and more about the location and surrounding area.

You can write the address below to find more information about the new location you are considering.

U.S. Chamber of Commerce
1411 K Street, NW, Suite 500
Washington DC 20005-3404

Newspaper & Yellow Pages

You could also subscribe to the local newspaper from the area you wish to live. Take into thought that local real estate brokers will mail you brochures about the area.

You can evaluate the hiring opportunities and positions available in the area you hope to live in.

And another idea would be to look in the yellow pages of the local phone book to be sure your health care provider needs can be taken care of, educational facilities, any restaurants, entertainment options and to check out the competition with business before relocating.

Career Counselor

The yellow pages in the phone book will also uncover a listing for career counselors that might be able to help you in many areas of relocating and finding a job. Here are a few ideas:

♥ Career Counselor's have contacts within your field.

♥ They can assess your marketable skills for a career change.

♥ They have networking abilities.

♥ They can refine your cover letter, resume and interview skills.

Some career services offer the internet as a resource. At their office (sometimes for a fee) they will let you look up Career Search or One Source which are national and international computer databases available on CD Rom. Once there, you look up any city within a certain radius and all the job descriptions you type in that are available will show up on the screen.

Internet Look Up

America Online, Google and CompuServe are great search engines to help you find out what jobs are in the area you wish to relocate to. If you want to make sure you have an employment opportunity  waiting for you, instead of just assuming you will have that opportunity hovering over your head, here is what you can do to prepare ahead of time.

Search for jobs in the area you wish to move to by finding your search engine, my favorite is Google.com, and typing in the key word 'jobs' and the city you wish to move to. Put these key words in 'parenthesis' to get a more specific look-up started. You should get quite a good start for researching job opportunities in a search like this.

Check newspapers online, too. They have launched a program called CareerPath.com which is an online interactive employment service listing jobs. This service will match up the employers with the employees!

How Much to Spend

This is different for each individual. Price is the result of demand any where you go and whatever you buy. The most important questions to ask yourself is what can you afford and is it what you will be happy with? Price can't always determine happiness. You are the only judge of what is right for you and your family.

> "In a city, (people's) huge number ensures that it will not only be more crowded than other places, but also more restrictive, competitive, bureaucratic, hectic, and just plain arousing; the quietest times in New Yorkers' apartments are louder than the noisiest in small towns."
>
> -Winifred Gallagher

Space

Take a walk through the home you are viewing and be sure there is enough space for you and your family. You don't have to buy a smaller house, you can actually give yourself room for growth and keep the extra room or two closed off at no cost until you need it. If you can meet all your needs without expensive renovations and remodeling then I suspect you will be happy in your new home. Ask these questions when you walk through:

- Will the house meet your space requirements?
- Does it meet your need for privacy?
- How about space for work or hobbies?

Look Over the Exterior

If you stand back from the house and look at it closely from all angles, does the house lean to one side or seem out of alignment? If yes, get a closer look and find out why.

Some old houses don't hold up to the weather after so many years. Or it could be the foundation, termites or dry rot, too. Check the foundation for cracks. If you see hairline cracks then it's probably okay, but if you see large cracks then the structure may need major work.

If you find foundation problems and still really want the house, I would hire a contractor to assess the actual damage costs and then try to negotiate the repairs into the buying of the house.

Drainage

You should also check for drainage problems around the base of the house. Excess water can cause a lot of problems under a building. The soil can weaken under the foundation and excess moisture can create wood rot and mold in those areas under the house.

Climate

Those wanting warmth all year will require different priorities than those wishing to watch the seasons change.

Part-time farmers will seek one sort of land while weekend adventurers will seek another. Do you want neighbors or wish for isolation?

Do you want a garden? Do you want a valley without trees? If you want to be a little more self sustaining then you will need a garden. Make sure the ground and climate will allow for the things you want in a garden.

Depending where you choose to live there could be drought or floods. Keep this in mind when you choose where to live.

"I cannot conceive the Spring of lands that have no Winter. I take my Winter gladly, to get Spring as a skeen and fresh experience."

-The Odd Farmwife, 1913

Family and Friends

When moving away from family and friends you need to determine your comfort zone for distance. How far do you want to travel to visit your family or friends? It could be that you find your new home is 500 miles from the ones you became accustomed to seeing on a weekly basis. It would be smart to determine a balance for the distance apart from family and friends that you are comfortable with.

Take into consideration that parents get older and need their children more. Sick relatives might want visits more often before they leave the earth. And healthy relatives like visits more often as they grow older, too.

For yourself, age makes a huge difference in the outcome of your surviving a move to the country. There are things in the country that are too much work to ask of a retired or older person. And I'm not being testy either; I'm being realistic. What you could do at 30, you could easily do at 40 with a little less jump to your step, but at 50 on up you should take your age into consideration before making the leap.

Also consider including the extended family in your moving and farming adventures. What you aren't able to do on the farm - couldn't your younger son or nephew do for you? Joel Salatin says it best in his book *You Can Farm,* "The people in your life undoubtedly will be your most important resource. Be sure to itemize the varied talents and assets each can bring to the venture so you will not overlook that resource."

Choosing Your Vehicle

There are many considerations when choosing a vehicle for the country. First of all, you should know the terrain of the area you choose to live in.

"Do nothing in great haste, except catching fleas and running from a mad dog."

-The Old Farmer's Almanac, 1811

Is it rugged? Does it have wash board part of the year? Are there holes and ruts to deal with? Does the county take care of the road? Does the county plow the road in the wintertime? Is the road a seven mile primitive dirt road, or paved smooth as silk?

Keeping the above things in mind, you might consider the following options in a vehicle:

- ♥ Four wheel drive
- ♥ Six to eight ply tread on the tires
- ♥ Winch for front end of truck
- ♥ Air conditioning if your weather warrants
- ♥ Used truck for hauling equipment, hay or feed for animals, etc

- ♥ Second car with good mileage for long hauls
- ♥ Spare tires on hand
- ♥ Fix a flat (tire) spray
- ♥ Survival Kit in vehicle
- ♥ Battery cables

Changing Wardrobe

There does seem to be a need to change your wardrobe after moving to the country. It depends on what part of the country you move to and what time of the year it is when you get there.

After leaving the city where everyone wears a suit and tie or a dress to work, it will seem funny to wear that sort of outfit while pulling weeds or clearing brush from the land in the mountains.

Research to find out which clothes will be suited best for you in your new location. It will save you hundreds of dollars if you are well prepared before starting the shopping spree.

I have become accustomed to wearing Levi jeans, a colored t-shirt and cowboy boots. These are my normal daily trimmings. I have one pant suit and a dress in the closet for big business events.

Number of Acres

When deciding on the number of acres you wish to own in the country remember to calculate animals you will raise and the minimum number of acreage they need to forage on.

Example: One cow will need 5 acres of nutritional pasture. If you plan to own an entire herd of cattle, you need to buy many more acres to cover their needs (of course this depends on the climate). If the habit of the living area is to rain and flood, or there are long periods of drought, then you will need to plan accordingly.

If, on the other hand, you are planning to own a small home and live all by yourself with no animals to keep you company or fill your dinner table - which is almost unheard of in my house - then you would get by just fine on one acre of land.

Easements/Access to Property

Check with the county clerk to be sure you agree with any easements that might allow folks to drive down the middle of your property. Also make sure you have year-round access to the property. Don't rely on a neighbors' word to always allow you through. Disputes will happen and the neighbor could stop your access when this occurs.

On our farm we have an easement that allows folks who live past us to drive right down the middle of our property, past our barns and through our fields to get to their cabins. It was a decision we decided to live with because these neighbors live in the city and only visit their properties about twice a year. These of course were our best neighbors!

At the other end of our 40 acres we decided to allow new neighbors to run electric and phone through the corner of our property line. Since we don't use that end of our property often and the grass will grow over where the ground was dug up for their lines, we can live with this decision as well.

Ron built a cabin on the other end of our 40 acres, when we parted ways he decided to keep that property for his future use. The neighbors up at that end asked him if he minded if they built a fence on his property to pen their horses in and he said 'Sure. Go ahead." Now the neighbors will have a fence to keep their horses in, along with the use of property right next to their own, and Ron will have a fence built at no cost to him. Everyone wins in this situation.

Think long and hard and be sure you can live with any decisions you make like the above mentioned ones. It is a choice you can't say 'yes' to and then take away when you don't like the end results.

Power to Property

It is highly recommended to have access to power at one corner of the property line if there is not an easier access to it. It is expensive to run power for a long distance.

The power company may only need to run the electric lines one mile from the nearest power line near your property, but they also charge you by the foot to return that line to the closest power station. These costs can add up considerably ....and quickly.

In our neck of the woods it cost our neighbors $27,000 to run the power line less than one mile from their home! And they took the shortcuts right through the woods and up the hills.

If you need to run electric very far from your property line make sure you budget for this cost.

Phone Available

As with power access it is advisable to make sure you can get a phone installed if you plan to have one at all.

Also if you're going to need or you want to have more than one phone line in your house, check with the local phone company to be sure they are set up for this option. When we moved up on the mountain the phone company hadn't updated the phone lines in this area for over 20 years. We could only get one phone line.

It took six weeks for the phone company to update and add more lines. Of course some of our neighbors had been waiting for over three years to get more phone lines in their homes. The phone company won't go through the expense of adding more lines to the entire  neighborhood unless there is sufficient need in the area. So, depending on where you choose to live, you might have a bit of a wait for extra phone lines, and in some cases you could have to wait for even one house phone line!

Now we have three phone lines for our home, business and internet needs. Here's what we do: The first phone line is for the house use, the second phone line is used for our business use and the third line is used for faxes and using the internet in the daytime (so we don't tie up the business line) and this last line is also used for my teenagers after five o'clock each night.

Water

Don't neglect to find out if water is available! You can live without shelter, clothes and cosmetics, but you can only live three days without water. Is there a well on the property? Does the well work properly? How many gallons per minute does it provide? How deep is the well? Is it hand dug or drilled from a professional?

If no well is found, do you have the funds to pay for a new one? Costs can vary from $3000 to $15,000 and if there are problems it could cost more.

Make sure you have budgeted for a well if there isn't one on your property. Remember if you plan to live there full time you will also need a septic tank and drain field. And of course, be sure the ground is potable so you are able to build the drain field.

Another thing you can do if there is no well on the property and you are putting one in yourself is get in touch with a witcher. I know it sounds strange to suggest using a witcher but if you find a reputable witcher who guarantees their work it really is an asset!

When our 14 foot hand dug well dried up we called a recommended witcher. Our witcher walked around with a metal tool in his hand and when the tool shook up and down uncontrollably, he told us that spot was where the water was waiting under the ground.

We were told exactly where to dig, approximately how deep the well digger would have to dig before he found water and at what angle to tell the well digger to dig.

We were guaranteed that the well digger would be within ten feet of the predicted depth of water and if there was no water found then we would be refunded our $500.

I was pretty skeptical over this procedure but since they had a guarantee for their work, my husband and I went for it and the well digger hit the water at an eight foot difference of his prediction and we now get between five and seven gallons of water per minute. This is more than we will ever use. If you hire a witcher ask them if they guarantee their work.

The reason I suggest this is because it saved us hundreds, maybe even thousands of dollars. When a well digging company comes up to dig a well on your property they don't know where the water is. They could dig six huge holes on your land before they find water and even then it might not be a continuous source of water.

Well diggers charge by the hour and by the foot dug; so it makes no sense for them to learn to do a witcher's job. Take this advice; hire a witcher.

> "There is absolutely no reason for being rushed along with the rush. Everybody should be free to go very slow."
>
> -Robert Frost

 If there is already a well established on the property, run the taps. Does the water flow steadily when a few taps are turned on at the same time? Is it fresh and smelling good? How about the taste? In the country you don't have the chlorine and bleach which is used in city water.

Remember, it is advisable to have the water tested no matter where you live or what someone else tells you about how safe and great tasting the water is. Visit your local health department and they will give you a container to send a sample of water in for testing.

One reason I would suggest this testing is if you have a shallow hand dug well on the property. Maybe there were cows or a pig pen close by the hand dug well and the droppings could have soaked into the ground; and therefore the droppings can seep into your water source! Do you really want to drink water that has feces in it? I know you don't want to take the chance of you or your family getting e-coli from your own water.

Also if you are bottle feeding a baby and you use the water for that feast to your child, then it is important to have the water tested before proceeding.

Another Water Option

Is there a creek near by? Is the creek water running part time or full time? Or are you willing to haul the amount of water you need in to the property once a week?

We had some friends who lived off the grid for many years. They ran solar with batteries and didn't have to do without a television, dishwasher, lights or electricity. Our friends were an older couple and the wife loved her flowers for their yard in the spring and summer months. During these times of the year her husband hauled in 300 gallons of water *every week* so she could water her flowers!

Make sure any decisions like the above ones that you make are worth living with. The man mentioned was the exception when it comes to going out of your way for a woman's needs. I don't suggest assuming your husband is the exception. Make sure all the decisions you make for your family are mutual agreements.

Zoning Laws

Check with the local zoning agency to be sure you will be allowed to use, build on and prepare your land in any manner you intend.

Also find out if a no-residential zoning district adjoins the new property or is uncomfortably close to the property. The location of nonresidential zoning districts near single family homes will influence the value and resalability of your home and the quality of life.

A critical source for information is the subdivision and land development plan. This plan will indicate how many homes will be developed or already exist in the area of your new home.

It would be a shame to buy property, start building and have the most beautiful home on the block when all of a sudden they start building an apartment building or small businesses next door. It happens!

Eminent Domain

Many public agencies have the right to condemn land for roads, drainage canals, schools, power lines, etc. It would be wise to check with the local planning board to find out if any such ideas are being contemplated.

Title Search

Ask for a title company to check records and be sure you are buying land which is free and clear of liens or encumbrances. Sometimes the person you are dealing with isn't as trustworthy as they seem.

I knew someone in the past who took a deep penalty from his 401K at work in order to buy 20 acres for retirement property. He didn't get a title search because he trusted the man he was dealing with.

After paying $22,000 cash to the man for a 20 acre piece of property, and looking forward to having the bonus of a 16' x 16' cabin structure put up on the new property, my friend was devastated to find out the man he had trusted with his money went bankrupt. My friend might have retrieved some of his loss but the man he had trusted with his 401K savings had also sold that same piece of property to thirty other people!

Pay the money and get a title search. This is only to protect yourself and your family from a loss that could affect your future.

Property for all Seasons

If possible, try to view the property in all four seasons. It makes perfect sense that some land will fare better in winter than other land. Land needs to be sloped properly to drain. Poorly sloped land creates pot holes and mud problems in the early spring when the snow has melted.

Do you want a garden? Then check to be sure you can get the south sun in the climate you want to plant.

In our neck of the woods we couldn't grow corn, melons or any long season growing garden goodies. It was terrible. There would be a short freeze in August and another in September and all the potatoes and beans would turn brown and wither off and die a week later. I was crushed each time but I kept trying.

It would be best to ask local neighbors what they can grow on their land; and don't think you can do better. Either live with the news or move some where else that has more options.

Mineral and Timber Rights

The seller may already have sold the timber and mineral rights to an earlier buyer. This is legally binding. Check the county records to make sure you will own the mineral and/or timber rights to the property you wish to buy if this is an option you wish to have with your new property.

Usually this isn't a big deal anyway. I mean, how often is it that someone finds a dinosaur bone or a diamond on your property and starts the excavation truck digging up holes all over the place?

If you don't mind someone else owning the rights to your land, then it won't be an issue unless that owner comes back wanting to dig up your property. I've not heard of this being a problem.

Southern Exposure

Do you wish to take advantage of the southern exposure? Then make sure there is some!

Yes, you can knock down some trees if they are in your way but if there is a mountain in the way of the proposed building site then you might want to look at another location.

These days southern exposure is so important when trying to become more self sufficient that I would suggest being really picky about the property you choose to buy. Be sure the property has all of your needs for future use of southern exposure.

Natural Hazards

All sorts of natural hazards can sharpen the mood in this world. When relocating, you need to be sure you can handle any natural hazards that are common for that area.

This includes blizzards or hurricanes if you are close to the ocean, droughts out in southern America and lots of rain in northern America.

Timber for Future Growth

When looking to buy property, why not buy land that has lots of trees? Later when they are marketable you can use the timber to pay off that years taxes or build a new barn. Remember that Gene Logsdon suggests that you plant new trees every ten years to replace any trees that you cut down. He uses his own timber to build his farm barns and sheds.

Want to build your home from your own trees? Trees needed for suitable logs should be the best, not mediocre.

If you plan to heat with wood you should determine how many cord of wood you would need per month or year. This may range between 1-10 cord depending on your climate and on the efficiency of your homes insulation, and type of wood burner you select to use.

"5-10 acres of woodland (properly managed) can be enough to provide a perpetual supply of wood fuel for your home", says Gene Logsdon.

Wood Stove

If you live in the mountains the chances are you will depend on a wood stove. After living on our mountain for five years I have come to the conclusion that it would have behooved us even more to invest in an old fashioned cook stove. I'd buy the kind that works as a stove to cook and bake in and also to burn wood in to warm the house.

Right now we own an old barrel shaped wood stove that heats up our entire two story three bedroom home. Our wood stove works even when the power goes out, so we are always warm. See my section on 'Transfer Switches' for more about when the power goes out.

Cook Stove

There are a few good reasons for a cook stove. If you lose power during a storm (which could last for days), you will still be able to cook and keep your family warm. And you can use your cook stove on a permanent basis to save on electric bills.

If you have a wood stove or a cook stove, you will need to bring in enough chopped wood for the winter months. See the next section on 'Collecting Wood'.

Our home uses six cord of wood a year for heating. We do not have floor base heat. There is no furnace even set up in our home. We totally and completely rely on a wood stove to keep us warm all year long.

The first winter on this mountain our families wondered if we would freeze to death. They did not think a wood stove could keep our entire three bedroom home warm enough. But I'm here to tell you that we were shoving blankets to the floor before each night was over! A wood stove can be a huge blessing and will keep your entire family warm without the monthly cost of a heating bill.

Collecting Wood

 If you decide to buy a wood stove or a cook stove, you will need to collect enough wood to last through the year. It is cheaper to get a permit and cut your own firewood in the forest, then split and stack the logs when you have time.

If you choose to buy your logs already split and delivered to your home, remember there are certain times of the year that it is cheaper to buy firewood in bulk. If you wait until the middle of winter you could pay much higher prices. Usually the best time of year for purchasing firewood is in the summer months.

As the saying goes, wood warms you two times. Once when you cut it and a second time when you burn it. By cutting your own firewood you will get exercise, warmth and the pleasure of a wood fire later.

If you have the time, gathering your own wood can save you large amounts of money. It can cut your yearly heating bill by three quarters.

- ♥   1 acre = 2/4 cord of hard wood each year.
- ♥   1 cord = 4' tall x 4' wide x 8' long stack of wood.
- ♥   10 acres should harvest 6 cord a year which would heat a three bedroom house.

Remember: Replace what you take to ensure future use!

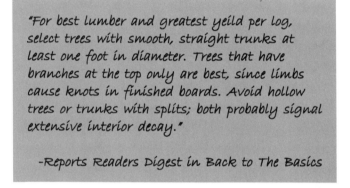

"For best lumber and greatest yeild per log, select trees with smooth, straight trunks at least one foot in diameter. Trees that have branches at the top only are best, since limbs cause knots in finished boards. Avoid hollow trees or trunks with splits; both probably signal extensive interior decay."

-Reports Readers Digest in Back to The Basics

Fences

If you need to build fences there are many books to help you in that chore. And you can also get a ton of information online.

There are many types of fences you can build. Since I believe in wooden fences and posts I will give you some tips on choosing wood for building your fences.

Life Expectancy of Fence Posts

Wood	Untreated	Treated
Birch	2-4 years	10-20 years
Cedar	15-20 yrs	20-30
Douglas Fir	3-7	15-18
Elm	4	15
Oak	5-10	15-20
Pine	3-7	20-30
Redwood	10-15	20-30
Spruce	3-7	10-20

Buildings

Plan for buildings and barns. Cows need a three sided structure to stand under during the worst of weather. Calves need a place free of drafts and rain. Pigs need an enclosed area to keep themselves out of the snow and rainy weather. Pigs do not do well in cold climates. Goats should be sheltered more adequately and their kids need to be kept completely free from drafts.

Remember to plan for future growth when you decide how big to build your buildings, sheds, barns, etc. In the future you may need more room in the shed.

Instead of building two 12' x 12' sheds, why not build one 12' x 24' shed to begin with? Give yourself room to grow! You don't want to end up with 40 small buildings all over your farm.

> *"It will not always be summer: build barns."*
> —Hesiod

Planning to Farm the Land

Not all soil is equal. Some folks think it is obvious that rural soil is just better than the soil in the city. Not always so. There are differences.

If you are planning to work the land and grow crops of any sort then you should check with the county extension agent and get a sample of the soil tested before buying the property. The county extension office will run a soil analysis report for you.

> *"Remember that agriculture is the best of engaged in an employment that would not disgrace a king."*
> —The Old Farmer's Almanac, 1836

Basements, Atticks & the Roof

Before agreeing to buy a new home in the country you should make sure to check for the basics. Look at the ceilings and lower walls in basements and atticks for water spots. This could indicate leaks in the roof. Ask the seller lots of questions. The only stupid question is the one you didn't ask.

To protect yourself further, you can stipulate in the papers before agreeing to buy the house that you will pay for an inspection to be sure the roof is not failing or leaking, but if the roof isn't in good health the seller will have to replace it before you will buy. This way you will not get stuck with the bill for installing a new roof on the house if it needs one.

Electricity

Check for signs of obvious problems such as old wiring, new wiring that looks messy, flickering lights or a lack of wall outlets.

If looking at an older home, you will probably be best off hiring a professional to check over the system to be sure it is safe before buying.

Fireplace

Is there a fireplace in the house? Look inside it to see if the bricks are in good condition. You don't want loose bricks which will need new grout. Watch for cracks in the bricks and crumbling -which should all be replaced as soon as possible if you buy the home.

If you are serious about buying this particular home, ask if you can start a fire to see that the draw works properly and the fireplace doesn't fill the house with smoke. Remember to open the damper first!

Plumbing

You can do a quick check of the plumbing by flushing the toilet, running the sink water and the shower at the same time. This will give you an idea of what kind of water pressure you have in the house.

Heating the House

It is essential for you to check the type of heating system offered in the home. Also ask the seller the age of the system and its state of repair.

Annual Heating Bill

It isn't uncommon these days to request a copy of the sellers annual heating bill costs. This will give you a good idea of the costs for heating and cooling the home on a yearly basis.

With a yearly sight of what your heating and cooling costs are projected to be, you can make a monthly budget work for your family needs.

And if the costs are much too high for what you determine is a good monthly bill amount, then you can look some where else to buy a home where you will be happy with the monthly bills.

Septic Tank

It is very common in the country for septic tanks to have drainage. The waste will flow into the tank underground where bacteria will break down the solids. The waste water will flow into a leach field with pipes to distribute it over a large area. A good system can last up to twenty years in this fashion if well maintained.

> *"You don't live longer in the country. It just seems that way."*
>
> -Dick Syatt

Pest Inspection

 Another good idea would be to get a pest inspection done on a house that you are definitely wanting to own. A simple check like this could save you thousands of dollars later.

Can you imagine buying an old farm house, moving in and renovating till your wealth is all in the house and then finding out that termites have eaten their way into the walls and porches? What would you do then? Protect yourself with an inspection if the house is older or if the house looks like it might have a pest problem.

Chat with Neighbors

Like always, the neighbors can be a good source of information that the seller may not wish to share with you. Go door to door and chat with them. Ask:

♥ about the road conditions in the winter

♥ about the road conditions in the spring

♥ does the county plow after it snows

♥ about wash-board if there is a dirt road involved

♥ how often does power go out and how long does it take for the electric company to repair the lines

♥ do they get a lot of strangers doing drive-by's in the area (to determine how safe the road is for you)

♥ ask about the amount of iron in the water so you can decide if you would need to invest in a water softening system

The more questions you ask now the less likely it will be that you are surprised when a problem arises later.

"We didn't have much, but we sure had plenty."
-Sherry Thomas

Abandoned Farm House

Have you considered buying an abandoned farm house? There are millions of them along the country-side and the owners would probably be glad to sell you theirs since the houses usually haven't been lived in for years.

Another plus for buying an abandoned farm house would be that the out buildings are already there. They built buildings to last back in the olden days. You wouldn't have much to do to get them up to par and workable. There might even be fences in place.

Yes, there would be considerable renovation to get it up and liveable, but the mortgage (if any) would be lower than buying a new house in the country or having your own built. This way you could be mortgage free a lot sooner.

Country Remedies

Taken from David Larkin's book *Country Wisdom*, these are country remedies printed exactly as he laid them out in his book. David Larkin does mention that these remedies should be relished for their interest, rather than heeded.

Abscess or Boil

♥ Tie bread in a white cloth, dip it in boiling water and place on the abscess overnight.

♥ Press a cabbage leaf dipped in hot water on the abscess.

♥ Cover the area with a slice of onion and wrap with a clean cloth.

♥ Apply a poultice made of crushed burdock leaves, or one made of ginger and flour, to draw boil to a head.

Bruises

♥ Treat a bruise by applying brown paper coated with molasses.

♥ Ease the pain by rubbing with an onion.

♥ Bath with an infusion of hyssop leaves.

Burns

♥ Honey applied to burns will help the pain and prevent blisters from forming.

♥ Soak a soft cloth in cod-liver oil and place it on the burn.

♥ Mix corn meal with powdered charcoal and add milk to make a paste for the burn.

Colds

♥ When a cold is coming on, put blackberry cordial in

a mug and top it with hot
water. Drink the cordial
in bed and go to sleep.

♥ Drink hot milk with
crushed garlic in it.

♥ Spread goose grease on
brown paper and put it on
your chest.

Corns

♥ Bind on bread soaked in
vinegar to remove corns.
Reapply mornings and
evenings.

♥ Burn willow bark and
then mix the ashes with
vinegar and apply to the
corn.

♥ Insert the toe in a lemon.
Keep it on during the
night. The corn can then
be easily removed.

Coughs

♥ Slice an onion very thin
and alternate layers of
onion and sugar. Place a

plate on top to weigh them down. The juice that forms is soothing for a cough and safe for children.

♥ Chop two large turnip roots into small pieces and boil in a quart of water. Cool and strain. Add an amount of honey equal to whatever portion is taken.

♥ Take a spoonful of kerosene mixed with sugar.

Cramps

♥ Cramps in the neck or legs can be relieved by an application of whiskey and red pepper.

♥ Drink warm pennyroyal tea.

♥ Tie periwinkle stems around the leg or arm that is likely to be affected.

Cuts and Wounds

♥   Remove the inside skin or coating from the shell of an uncooked egg. Place its moist side on a cut to promote healing.

♥   Bath the cut in a solution of water and baking soda. Sprinkle it, while still wet, with black pepper.

♥   Cover a large cut with cow dung which is soft and creates heat. The cut will heal quickly.

♥   Apply cobwebs to stop cuts from bleeding.

♥   Press yarrow leaves to a cut to stop the flow of blood.

♥   Use a moist wad of chewing tobacco as a poultice.

Diarrhea

- ♥ In the summer eat fresh blackberries or boil blackberries in water, strain and drink the liquid.

- ♥ Stew up garden rhubarb with some sugar and eat a spoonful as long as necessary.

- ♥ A tablespoon of W.I. rum, a tablespoon of molasses and the same quantity of olive oil, well simmered together is helpful for this disorder.

- ♥ Flour boiled thoroughly in milk, so as to make quite a thick porridge is good.

Earache

- ♥ To alleviate the slight ear ache, blow pipe or cigarette smoke into the ear.

- ♥ To cure an earache, insert a piece of hot onion into the ear.

- ♥ Put a few drops of hot sweet oil (olive oil) into the ear and plug with cotton.

Eyes

- ♥ Black eyes can be eased by using a grated apple poultice.

- ♥ Sore eyes can be treated with an eye wash made of apple juice.

- ♥ Soak bread in a little milk and tie over the eye and leave over night to relieve inflammation.

- ♥ To help soreness, apply fresh green plantain leaves to the eyelids.

- ♥ Cure a sty by putting grated potatoes, covered by a cloth, on the eye.

Feet

♥ For offensive odor, soak feet in water in which green bark of oak has been boiled.

♥ For excessive perspiration, put bran or oatmeal into the socks.

♥ To relieve itching feet, soak every day in cider vinegar.

Fever

♥ Pound horseradish leaves into a pulp. Apply to the soles of the feet to draw out fever.

♥ Break a fever by drinking hot ginger tea.

♥ Put slices of raw potato on the forehead to draw out a fever.

Hair

♥ To make hair thicker, massage the juice of watercress into the scalp.

♥ To get rid of dandruff, massage vinegar into scalp several times a week.

Hay Fever

♥ Steep rose petals in a cup of hot water. Strain and apply drops to the eyes during the day to relieve irritation.

♥ Mix leaves and flowers of goldenrod and ragweed. Put one-half ounce of the herbs in two cups of boiling water and allow to steep for ten minutes. Drink a small glassful four times a day to cure hay fever.

Headaches

♥ Drink chamomile tea to soothe the head.

♥ Bath the forehead with hot water in which mint or sage has been boiled.

♥   Cure a headache by swallowing a spider web.

♥   Soak a cloth in warm vinegar and apply to the forehead.

Poison ivy or oak

♥   Mix powdered lime with lard until you have a paste and spread on the rash.

♥   Apply milk, heavily salted to skin affected by poison ivy. Allow to dry.

♥   Slit the stem of jewel weed, and rub its sticky juice directly on the skin and let dry. When it starts to itch, reapply.

♥   Squeeze the milk from the stems of milkweed and apply it to the rash.

♥   Juice squeezed from the leaf of the elderberry and applied directly to the inflamed area will relieve the itch. Continue until the rash is gone.

Rheumatism and Arthritis

♥ Keep rheumatism away by carrying a potato in the pocket, unseen by the opposite sex. The smaller and harder it becomes, the less likely the suffering from rheumatism.

♥ Rub the aching limb with oil and mustard.

Sore Throat

♥ Gargle with warm, salt water.

♥ Drink hot sage tea.

♥ Gargle with warm tea made from slippery elm bark.

Stings and Bites

♥ Rub the spot with mashed plantain leaves.

- ♥ Dab bee stings with household ammonia.

- ♥ Rub dock leaf on insect stings, and also on needle stings.

Stomach

- ♥ Eat fresh mint or drink mint tea to settle an upset stomach.

- ♥ Drink chamomile tea for an upset stomach.

- ♥ Place crushed horse-radish leaves directly on the skin over the stomach for itching.

Teeth

- ♥ To relieve a toothache, chew the leaves of catnip.

- ♥ Treat toothache by putting a clove in the tooth, or using clove oil.

Warts

- ♥ To remove warts, rub them with green walnut.

Part III
Now That You Are Home

THE BIRTHPLACE

Here further up the mountain slope
Than there was ever any hope,
My father built, enclosed a spring,
Strung chains of wall round everything,
Subdued the growth of earth to grass,
And brought our various lives to pass.
A dozen girls and boys we were.
The mountain seemed to like the stir,
And made of us a little while --
With always something in her smile.
Today she wouldn't know our name.
(No girl's, of course, has stayed the same.)
The mountain pushed us off her knees.
And now her lap is full of trees.

-Robert Frost

Trading Your Sweat for Labor

Neighbors in the country are usually more than willing to pull together and barter for the services of others. Let your neighbors know what you have to barter with and what it is you would like done in return.

Do you want a shed built? You'll buy the materials but you want a contractor to put it together? Well, let your neighbors know this and one of them might be a contractor who builds things. Maybe he needs a tractor for a project he's doing on his property. Do you own a tractor? Are you willing to trade your time or tractor in return for the time of the contractor building your shed?

Can you offer the use of your truck to a neighbor who needs to bring in a few loads of cut firewood and will in return bring you a load of firewood? You can see how bartering can really save you a lot of money!

I know folks in the country who raise a pig a year in return for the orchard owners grounded-apples. The orchard owner can't use the apples since they are rotten or bruised from falling to the ground. So he delivers these apples to the pig owner in return for a pig that is butcher weight. He then has the pig butchered and gets enough meat for his family table for a year. And all he did was barter with unsalable apples!

Can you think of things you can do to barter with neighbors? First, think of all the talents or tricks of the trade you know for your profession and list them on paper. Now, sit down and decide what you want done with your property. What do you want to build? What do you want to grow? What tasks do you need to achieve in order to accomplish these goals? List them all.

The last thing you need to do is keep that list handy and mention these things to your neighbors when you talk to them. Mention what your talents are and offer to trade those talents for the help you need from others. People like to trade sweat for labor. Money is a lot harder to come by than sweat is!

Off the Grid

If you live off the grid then you must decide in what way you receive the power to charge batteries for your solar needs. A good quality propane or diesel generator would work wonders for charging batteries.

Take this advice and do not buy a cheap generator. Remember that this investment will determine your happiness in the future of your home needs and desires. Invest wisely now.

If you have a 400 gallon propane tank put on your property you can run the stove, refrigerator, washer & dryer (anything that runs on propane) and the propane truck company will come up to your home twice a year to fill the propane tank for you.

This sort of investment would cost less in the long run, is more energy efficient and is more self-sufficient. It all depends on what your needs are.

Generator

For a back up power source I think every home should have a generator. One time when we lived in Auburn, Washington we lost our electricity for nearly a week. If you live in the city you know how hard that can be for a person, and I had two little kids. We bought our first generator that week and it's been an excellent source of reassurance ever since.

And I don't recommend buying an over-used or cheap generator either. I'd buy a nice quality propane generator that can and will hold up to nasty weather and lots of use. This way you will be covered in the event of electrical emergencies.

"Whatever you can do or dream you can, begin it. Boldness has genius power and magic in it."

-Goethe

Think Solar or Propane

Now that you live in the country you can try to become more self-sufficient as time allows. When appliances need to be replaced, find out about investing in a propane stove, washer and dryer, even a hot water heater can be propane these days.

Not only is using propane better for the environment it is more efficient in a lot of cases.

Transfer Switch Bonus

We installed what is called a transfer switch. This is easily put in by an electrician and draws electricity from the generator when the power goes out to bring electricity into your house.

You can usually only run a few rooms, depending on the generator strength and a few other factors, but it's well worth the cost. I think we paid about $400 to have our transfer switch installed.

When we lose power in our area we can still run electricity in up to six rooms of our home. We usually run the kitchen and living room since these are the most important. Of course the electric stove or microwave would draw too much from a small generator. But the refrigerator is okay and our food will not go bad if the power is out for an extended amount of time.

Water Pump

One Christmas a friend of mine's dad bought him a hand pump for a hand dug well. I got to thinking about the awesome effects this hand pump could have in the country and here is my advice.

Buy one! Out in the country you might live off the grid or you might lose your electricity for a long amount of time. Sometimes it could take up to a week in the winter for the electric company to even find the source of why the electricity was lost in a remote area. And sometimes every single person in that area will think that someone else in the area will have called in the problem and so the electric company doesn't even know you have a problem!

A hand pump to create a water source is an excellent idea and a great way to ensure that your family is well taken care of in emergencies. You can't live without water.

Water Barrels

You know those big 50 gallon drums that are sitting around people's yards rusting? Try and find a clean one that you can store rain water in. You can use this water when the electricity goes out.

What I found out is that you don't need perfect water to replenish the toilet water, clean counters or even clean up for the day. If you didn't have a water source for an extended amount of time it would be great to just walk outside to where you store your barrel(s) and empty a few gallons into milk containers for household use.

You can read my extended notes on 'water' in Part II of this book, but I will touch on the subject here as well. Just a short story to give you a visual of what I am saying.

We lost the use of our hand dug well for approximately three weeks before we could have another one dug for us. At the time we had horses, cows, pigs, a goat, and various other animals, such as chickens and dogs.

Every single day we had to make sure every one of those animals had water to drink -even though we had no source of water for them! Did you know that a cow or horse can drink 12 gallons of water in a given day? This created a problem since we had no water at the time.

A neighbor was kind enough to let us draw water from his well and fill our 50 gallon barrels with water for these animals. Okay, that took care of the animals. What about flushing the toilet? You can't flush a toilet without at least three gallons of water.

I had to take empty gallon milk jugs to my mom's to fill with her water. We also used this for other bathroom uses, such as brushing our teeth. We just tipped the jug and used the water as sparingly as we could.

I explain it more in Part II, but you get the idea. Water is an essential in life and you have to accommodate for the time when it might not be available to you.

Keeping a Tractor

A lot of folks think you can live without the cost of a tractor. These are really rough people who work really hard day in and day out to keep their homes running.

After living on the mountain for five years, I have to disagree. We just couldn't have made it without our trusty 65' Ford. The hard work involved may be exhilarating to some folks, but those of us who want to enjoy the fruits of our labors will buy a tractor!

I sure don't want to be a slave to my property. Without a tractor to help us with the really heavy, hard work load, we would constantly be working and it wouldn't seem to me that we'd ever finish in time to sit back and drink a lemonade with the neighbors.

I completely recommend that you invest in a good used tractor if you plan to build any of your own buildings (tool shed, garden shed, outhouse, chicken coop, pig housing, barn, etc.) or need to clear any land. The time and energy you save is well worth the investment.

Over time you will find there are endless uses for a tractor. We used ours to fill garbage cans full of feed from our grain bin. Then we utilized the tractor to move the garbage cans close enough to each animals pen so we could easily feed them each day.

 In the winter there is a need to plow the roads so we can use the driveway. If we didn't have the tractor to plow for us, we would have to hire someone else to do this job.

The tractor comes in handy in late spring, too, when we need to knock down the ruts we've made after the snow melts and our driveway is muddy.

Implements for the tractor make it easy to mow lots of lawn fast (we have a five foot wide mower), dig deep holes (we have an auger for fence post holes), use a fork lift to unload from trucks, plow a garden spot and the tractor has lots of other uses as well.

My Take on Guns

Used for protection only guns are not the enemy. People who use them for ill needs or to harm another person are the ones who give guns a bad name. We have a couple of guns for specific uses and no one is allowed to use them for play. We keep the bullets locked up.

I recommend having everyone in the family take a class on how to handle a gun or rifle. It is very important that teenagers learn to respect such an instrument.

Our guns are used when we need to put an animal down. We don't want our livestock to suffer so we shoot them when it's necessary.

For those who just don't want to own a gun, I recommend a pepper spray that you take with you on hikes just in case you come in contact with a bear or cougar.

This pepper spray is like a regular pepper spray only much more powerful. It can stop a cougar or bear in their tracks from 60 feet away! To order your own pepper spray for the outdoors, visit the Universal Defense Alternative Products Industries online at: www.udap.com.

Keep a Survival Kit

I hope that everyone would have a survival kit in their home. No, this isn't the same thing as a first-aid kit. You should actually keep a second first-aid kit inside the survival kit. Most people who do this sort of thing have a survival kit in their home *and* in their car.

In the event of an emergency you would want to be prepared for your family needs. Maybe you only lose power for a day, but what if you lost it for a week? Do you have what it takes to care for your family for a week without electricity?

Of course, I am not a survival expert so I am just giving you the basic list of essentials. You would need to decide what other things to include. Think about your own individual family needs. Is someone taking medicine? Does someone need allergy kits? Keep this in mind when you pack your kits.

A simple list of things to keep in your house survival kit would be, but please add your own ideas, too:

- Can opener
- Canned foods
- High protein foods that don't rot
- Flash light
- Roll of toilet paper
- Warm blanket(s)

- 2 gallons of water
- First-Aid kit
- Sewing kit
- Medical needs for family members
- Things to keep little kids busy

A few ideas for a car emergency survival kit would include, but please, again, add your own ideas:

- Flash light
- Jumper cables
- Canned food w/pop up lids
- High protein bars
- Gallon of water
- Blanket(s)
- Warm gloves, hat & boots in winter
- Filled gas can
- Medical needs for family members
- Things to keep little kids busy

Consider Fire Protection

 It would be wise to find out where the local fire department is coming from. Can they make it to your home if there were a fire before it burned to the ground?

And is the fire department paid folks or volunteers? This could determine how quickly they would get to your home. Volunteers have to be rounded up first and then sent to the destination in need. Paid fire persons can leave as soon as the call comes in.

Gas Cans

I think it would be tremendously wise to keep extra gas cans on hand. You never know when your wife or husband will coast home on the car fumes in the hope that you can save them from disaster!

You can also have auto fuel on hand for generators if the power goes out, the lawn mower and other things that use auto fuel on the farm.

Use Low Wattage Light Bulbs

Every little bit helps when your income lowers from the move to the country. Using low wattage fluorescent light bulbs will not only help the environment, it will lower your utility bills. Costco has great deals.

> "It gives me such joy. It lifts me up --just like a door has opened into the past."
>
> -Ethel Wright Mohamed

Go without TV

Not everyone will agree on this scope of the cabin life. TV is a time consumer. If it is used wisely, perhaps at the end of the evening when all chores are finished, then it can be an asset.

But most folks watch a minimum of six hours of TV a day and that is a huge waist of time for anyone. Can you imagine how much work they could be finishing up with that extra six hours a day to do so with? It's amazing how much time we waste these days.

If it's absolutely necessary, like for your health or the lives of those around you if you don't have a TV present, then I suggest having rules and times it can be turned on. Such as when the chores are finished for the day.

Create an Instant Pantry

A small closet, or an extension of the laundry room can be made into a pantry so you can store extra cans of food, boxed foods and any jars you stock up on.

I store my canned jars in a dark closet at the bottom of the stairs that no one would use otherwise. We put extra supplies for my 'Awesome Big Cook' days in there too. When you buy in bulk a closet can be used to stock many items.

Shelf in Laundry Room as Pantry

You know those non-fancy sturdy plastic or metal shelves that Wal-Mart or other department stores carry? The ones with 3-5 shelves, they are cheap and provide lots of storage room? Yes, those ones.

Okay, buy a big unit, one that will fit in your laundry room and then you have an area to store extra food. I like to keep all the box items, canned foods and things you buy in bulk that keep well, in here. Remember that the laundry room is a wet, heated room most of the time so you can't store onions or things like that in there. Those things will eventually mold.

Install Shelves in Closets

You can never have enough storage room in any house. I find that installing shelves in coat closets and other closets can be an excellent asset. Otherwise those areas are usually just wasted space. Utilize them!

Even a shelf above the water heater for those hardly used items or tools that we all collect, helps. I keep my dust pan, broom and mop in here! I've even asked for a few smaller shelves to be added above the water heater so that I can store things I buy in bulk but don't use very often. Like my cleaning supplies.

Costco for Stocking Up

I love Costco! If you pay close attention you can really save time and money at Costco.

I stock up on many items and freeze them. I make  sure I only buy enough that my family will eat before it goes bad in the freezer, too. You don't want to buy three years worth of butter only to find that it was freezer burnt or lost its nutrition after six months.

Things for the freezer include twelve pounds of butter, two weeks worth of breads and any meats that you don't raise for your freezer.

Things for the pantry include green beans, corn, other veggies, soups, sauces, pastes, rice, etc. You get the idea. And then you can stock up on boxed foods such as stove top stuffing, pastas, noodles, cereals, etc. You can get great deals on tuna fish at Costco and white chicken chunks.

What about coffee and creamer? I don't drink coffee so I don't have to buy it anymore but when I was married

I used to buy six cans of coffee and three tubs of creamer. It would last him about eight months or so.

Then you have your paper products. Do you have room above the washer and dryer or above the coats in the hall closet to stuff a few extra bags of toilet paper, paper towels or napkins?

Don't forget about sugar and flour either. I buy a huge plastic containers that will store about 25 pounds of sugar and flour and then I buy the big bag at Costco and stock them in the containers for future use. No bugs can get in to harm or destroy my stock and we're all happy.

And for those special items we all have a habit of buying; don't be afraid to buy in bulk! If you like the little jar coffees, bottled water or your favorite beer, then buy a few cases of them to save you the time of coming back in a week to replenish your stock.

Personal Hygiene Stock Up

When you live in the city or the country it just makes more sense to buy in bulk so you don't need to replenish your shelves every week or every month.

I like to stock up on all the personal hygiene items my family uses all year long. I usually buy a large tupperware container with a lid and store these items on a shelf behind the towels or under the sink. You can put them where ever you find the room. Label the containers if you use more than one.

Stocking up makes perfect sense to me. Is there a sale on shampoo that you use? Buy 6-8 bottles! How about deodorant and toothpaste? I even buy extra tooth brushes for company that might have forgotten theirs.

Not only do you save money because you are buying these items in bulk when they go on sale, but you are also saving your auto fuel and especially your time. Instead of driving down to the store once a month, you are driving for these things only once a year!

Instead of buying one carton of q-tips, buy two or three and have enough for the year. I like to stock up on these items in the fall and that way I don't have to run around driving in the snow and ice just to find these things. And I always buy 4-6 bags of toilet paper. It doesn't last all year, not with four girls in the house, but it keeps me home longer.

Sometimes it won't make any sense for you to drive to town to buy toothpaste if you run out. If you buy eight boxes of it, then your family would be okay for a year.

In the fall, check the shelves or tupperware boxes and see what needs to be replenished. Then go buy that and you will be stocked up for another year!

Raise Your Own Food

Since I cover this subject area more in Part IV of this book, I won't go into great detail here. But to hit on the basics, I just want to mention that raising your own animals can have so much benefit for your family.

Did you know that one pound of hamburger from the grocery store can have up to 300 different cows mixed in it? It's true. If you raise your own animal and have it butchered and put in your freezer, then you will know what is in your meat and that it is healthy for your family to eat.

I realize that not everyone has room for an 800 pound cow, or a 500 pound pig, but you can usually talk a farmer into raising the animal for you at their place for a price. Maybe you can even barter for some of the cost.

You can do this with beef, pork, chicken, turkey, rabbit and duck. Just find the farmer who has it for sale and go from there.

If you haven't tasted fresh meat then you owe it to yourself and your family to give it a try.

Build Pens before Acquiring Animals

Build pens and fences before buying the animals to fill those pens. You should know exactly where you will keep an animal, how and what you will feed it, and what the animal's needs are *before* you bring it home.

Also, by starting slow when designing your yard and outside building desires, you will be making things a lot easier on the one who has to build it all.

Keeping Dogs

To alert you of intruders or wild animals I recommend owning a big dog that barks when something happens in the yard. A bonus will be that you can take the dog with you as a companion when you hike or go for a short walk. The dog can let you know when something is amiss.

Without a dog to bark at the things you won't hear out in your yard at night, you might get more visitors than you want. Our dog keeps coyotes at bay, raccoons are afraid to get too close to our chicken coop and we have a friend to go on a walk. Two big dogs are better than one. They can protect one another as well as keep each other company.

"Then suddenly, overnight, the orchard would burst into glorious bloom, filling the air with a sweet, tart, innocent fragrance."

-Marilyn Kluger

Build a Shed

One of the first things you'll probably want to build is a shed. When you move you can store the stuff you were keeping in the garage or hall closets in the new shed. And remember when I mentioned earlier about building a shed twice the size you think you will need in an effort to leave room for growth!

When we moved to the country we had a two car garage and three bedroom house full of crap and we didn't have any storage place to keep it all. The first thing we did was build a shed for storage.

We built a 12' by 24' shed and then we had a safe place for extra camping gear, etc. The extra size gave us room to later add our freezers, generator set up, 4-wheeler storage, and some tools.

Save Egg Cartons

You probably already do this if you have chickens laying eggs. If not, start saving the egg cartons while you live in the city because you can never have enough of these egg cartons once you own laying chickens. Especially if you decide to sell eggs to make money.

I can easily move three to five egg cartons a week to friends and family who want fresh eggs. I ask all of them to return the cartons for future use.

Selling Eggs

 One simple set up for the homestead would be a chicken coop. Almost every household buys eggs for their refrigerator once or twice a week.

After you are established in the area, it will be easy for folks to stop by after work and pick up their eggs for the week. You can post a notice at the local grocery store and bulletin boards around town to announce it.

Sell ½ a Cow

Depending on your climate, one cow requires approximately five acres to graze upon and keep the cow happy and healthy for the summer and fall months.

Raising a calf up to butcher weight is one of the easiest things to do. You can teach them about electric fencing and keep them in the fence line a lot easier.

Then it is only a matter of making sure they have water every day. It will be necessary to feed them hay if your pasture isn't sufficient in nutrients.

It takes a year to raise the calf to proper weight for butchering. In the meantime you log in all your costs. Keep track of it all. Then find a family member or a friend and ask if they want to split the cow meat with you. You can recoup your costs by selling half the cow to them. And you get to fill your freezer with beef too!

"If your town has a good doctor, encourage him in every way to stay -- especially by paying his bill promptly."

-The Old Farmer's Almanac, 1943

Country Household Hints

Taken from facts gathered by David Larkin in his book *Country Wisdom.* These country household hints were gathered from books published in the 19th century, such as *Mrs. Child's Frugal Housewife.* Here are some selected items of household advice that show how to keep things clean and sparkling in the country. Many of these natural cleaners are still effective and most are written just as they were back then. I'll put them in alphabetical order for you.

Baskets

♥ Apply equal parts of boiled linseed oil and turpentine to baskets to clean and prevent drying. Then wipe off excess with a dry cloth.

♥ To clean, first scrub with lye from the wash tub, and then rinse with strong salt water.

Brass

♥ Crushed course rhubarb leaves will clean both brass and copper.

♥ Mix equal parts of salt and flour and moisten with vinegar to make a thick paste. Apply with a damp cloth. Then wash and dry.

♥ Shine unvarnished beds with half a lemon dipped in salt. After washing and drying, rub the brass with rottenstone.

♥ Rottenstone and oil are propper materials for cleaning brasses. If wiped every morning with flannel and New England rum, they will not need to be cleaned half as often.

Brooms

♥ To make a new broom last longer, soak it in hot salt water before using.

Carpets

♥ Cut the heart of a cabbage in half. Using it like a brush, go over the carpet to clean.

♥ Coat grease spots with a layer of cornmeal, rub into the carpet and let stand overnight. Then brush up cornmeal.

♥ To sweep carpets clean, first sprinkle with fresh grass clippings or with fresh, dry powder snow.

♥ Clean a dirty carpet by scattering grated raw potatoes and then brushing vigorously.

Copper

♥ To remove tarnish, clean it with half a lemon dipped in a mixture of one tablespoon of salt and one tablespoon of vinegar.

♥ Dampen an old cloth and rub fine sand on the pieces until they gleam. Procure very fine sand from ant hills.

Dampness

♥   To reduce dampness in closets, wrap twelve pieces of chalk together and hang them up.

Fireplace

♥   When the fire is burning brightly, toss in a handful of salt to act as a cleaner.

♥   To remove soot and grit from inside the chimney, place a couple handfuls of common bay salt hay on the fire.

Floors

♥   Clean varnished floors and wood work with cold tea to bring out their shine.

♥   Before sweeping a dusty floor, sprinkle with damp tea leaves, or fresh grass cuttings. They will collect the dust and prevent it from rising onto the bedding and furniture.

Furniture

♥ To remove minor white marks from wooden furniture, rub with a paste made of olive oil mixed with cigar ashes. Then polish off with a soft cloth.

♥ To blend in small surface scratches, rub with the broken edge of a piece of walnut meat and polish with a soft cloth.

♥ Give a fine soft polish to varnished furniture by rubbing with pulverized rottenstone and linseed oil and afterwards wipe clean with a soft silk rag.

Glass

♥ Clean a glass bottle or decanter by filling with soapy water and adding a couple tablespoons of vinegar.

♥ Wipe crystals from chandelier with two parts

vinegar to three parts water, then rinse and dry.

Gold

♥ Polish gold by using a soft cloth and a paste made of cigar ashes and water.

Ice

♥ Put hay on icy steps in the winter to prevent slipping. Keep a bale beside the door you ordinarily use. It won't track into the house like ashes or salt.

Knives

♥ Clean and polish blades with fire place ashes.

Leather

♥ Clean leather by rubbing with equal parts of vinegar and boiled linseed oil and then polish with a cloth.

♥ Beat the whites of three eggs and rub them with a soft cloth into a leather

chair. The leather will soon
be clean and shine as if
new.

Odor

♥ Simmer vinegar on the
stove to get rid of unpleasant cooking odors.

♥ Put out a cut onion and
leave until it has drawn
unpleasant smells to itself
and then throw it away.

Paint

♥ Hardened paint on brushes
can be softened by soaking
in boiling vinegar. Afterwards wash in hot soapy
water.

♥ Remove paint from glass by
applying hot vinegar with a
cloth. After it is softened,
scrape off gently.

Pests

♥ To keep ants away from the
house, sprinkle dried and
powdered leaves of tansy
and pennyroyal on door
steps and window ledges.

♥ Freshly cut pennyroyal placed in a room, or drops of oil sprinkled about, will keep away mosquitoes.

♥ Tansy or pennyroyal will keep away fleas. Rub cats and dogs with fresh-cut pennyroyal once a week.

♥ A muslin bag filled with pounded cloves and placed on the pantry shelf will keep flour and grains free of weevils.

♥ To keep moths away, procure shavings of cedar wood, enclose in muslin bags and place in chests, drawers and closets with woolen cloth.

Pewter

♥ When polish is gone, first rub on the outside with a little sweet oil (olive oil) on a piece of soft linen; then clear oil off with pure whiting (chalk) on linen cloths.

Silver

♥   Soak tarnished silverware in sour milk for half an hour. Then wash in soapy water and dry.

♥   Soak tarnished silver in potato water for several hours.

♥   For scratches use a paste of olive oil and whiting and rub with a soft cloth.

Stains

♥   Moisten fruit stains with glycerine, let stand for several minutes and rinse.

♥   Hold fabric with stains from berries and juices over a basin and pour boiling water through. Then wash with soap and rinse.

♥   Dip clothing with fresh bloodstains in salted water, to remove or diminish stain.

♥ Tea-stained cloth should be rubbed with a mixture of one tablespoon of salt and one cup of soft soap and then placed outside in the sun for a day, before laundering.

Wallpaper

♥ Make a smooth paste of equal parts of cornstarch and water and rub on wallpaper spots. When it is dry, brush off and spots will be gone.

Windows

♥ To clean, rub down with kerosene on newspapers. Especially good for rain spots.

Part IV:

Making Money on the Homestead

A story about Thomas Edison as reported by his son, Charles:

"It is sometimes asked, 'Didn't he ever fail?' The answer is yes. Thomas Edison knew failure frequently. His first patent, when he was all but penniless, was for an electric vote-recorder, but maneuver-minded legislators refused to buy it.

"Once, he had his entire fortune tied up in machinery for a magnetic separation process for low-grade iron ore -- only to have it made obsolete and uneconomical by the opening of the rich Mesabi Range.

"But he never hesitated out of fear of failure. 'Shucks,' he told a discouraged co-worker during one trying series of experiments, 'we haven't failed. We now know a thousand things that won't work, so we're that much closer to finding what will.'"

What Do You Want To Do In The Country?

The biggest thing that holds folks back from making the move from the city to the country is the lack of jobs in the country. The truth is that most rural folks have to keep two or more jobs to make ends meet. But these are part time jobs or home office jobs that they most surely love and enjoy.

Since you will most likely be living on 50% less than your present income after moving to the country, there is some careful planning to do beforehand, but you don't have to let this decision stand in the way of your dreams. You can get a job at a store or other place in the country until you find the right job for your future, too. Either way, make plans, get the skills before you move, and go from there.

Says Les Scher author of *Finding & Buying Your Place in the Country,* "You make more money living in the city, but you spend it all going out to restaurants or shows to try to forget about the fact that you're living in the city. In Garberville, CA, where I live, I could go a whole week without taking my wallet out. In the city I can blow $300 without even thinking about it."

I guess the first thing you should do is sit down and decide what your talents are, what your schooling consists of, what you have to offer in the way of selling your projects or homemade gift items, your gardening skills, canning skills, automotive skills, computer skills, etc. Did you take advantage of my recommendation of completing a trade school class to add to your resume of skills in Part I of this book? You can learn other skills in the comfort of your home before you ever take a drive through the country meadows. This can prepare you to fare better once you live in the country.

Before I get down to the business of giving you country business suggestions, I would also like to remind you that if you do take a job in the small town you move to, remember that the newspaper doesn't list all the jobs available. Those ads are only the folks who advertise their business needs. Not every business can afford to list their needs with the paper.

So, walk in to a place you wish to work in and introduce yourself. Let the owner know you are moving, or have moved there already, and that you would love to work with them. Tell them why you want to work there and leave your resume in case an opening is free in the future.

Availability of Jobs in the Country

There might not always be the job you need when moving to the country. The ideal set up would be for you to learn a trade that you could do from your home office. This way you could be home for your family and children and still make a living.

Just a few ideas for home based jobs would be:

- Freelance Writer
- Medical Transcription
- Accounting
- Automotive Skills
- Business Management
- Bookkeeping
- Computer Programming
- Cooking & Catering
- Electrician
- Farrier (trimming horse shoes)
- Gardening/Landscaping
- Home Inspector
- Interior Decorating
- Internet Specialist
- Locksmithing
- PC Repair
- Private Investigator
- Real Estate Appraiser
- Sewing & Dressmaking
- Small Engine Repair
- Veterinary Assistant
- Writing articles for magazines and newspapers

Of course I don't recommend you quit your current job until you are sure you can make it at one of the above jobs. The thing is, if you took my advice in Part I of this book then you made sure you had a special trade skill that would help you acquire a job now.

For more information on any of the above subjects, just write your request to the following address and they will send you the data you need to get started in that trade.

Stratford Career Institute
PO Box 875
Champlain, NY 12919-9872

Possible Commute

Keep in mind the commute necessary depending on where you choose to live. The farther you are from the city, the more travel expenses you will require if you can't work from a home office.

MONEY

Of course this is just a sample. You will need to add categories where you see fit and remove the ones that don't apply to you.

Figure out your fixed expenses for living in the country. By using this worksheet you can see how much it will cost you to survive monthly in country life.

Housing	$
Utilities (gas, phone, elec.)	$
Food	$
Car expenses (insurance)	$
Credit cards	$
Car payment	$
Entertainment	$
Savings	$
Miscellaneous	$
New clothes	$
Lunches out	$

And remember that if you leave your spouse at home while you work all day, it is recommended that you do come home each evening to share in the work load. It could be too much for one person to run your country homestead. And this could hurt your relationship.

Run a Business From Your Home

As I mentioned above in the 'availability of jobs in the country', if your line of work involves a computer and you can set it up so that the telephone transfers most of your work, then you can work from home.

Did you know that when you work from home you can claim a percentage of the home costs as deductions? My home office is one-quarter of our home, so I can claim one-quarter of the house utility expenses as deductions on income taxes. It's quite the write off.

Maybe you are needed away from home for meetings once a week, or every other week but the commute is so much less so the expenses will drop.

Hobby or Working Farm

What will be considered a hobby farm? If you buy animals, raise them and make no profit, then you have a hobby farm. Now, if you are able to plan and market well, then you can consider it a working farm and the IRS will let you make considerable deductions.

Of course, you do get the first three years to find out if you are a hobby farm or a working farm. Just keep all your receipts and even if you don't make a profit you can still claim deductions on your income taxes. After three years the IRS will ask that you show a profit to keep deducting on a regular basis.

> "We are American farmers ...Our grandsires freed this virgin continent, plowed it from East to West, and gave it to us. This land is for us and our children to make richer and more fruitful."
>
> -Farm Journal

What Can You Sell?

You might need to do some market research in your area before deciding what to invest in or sell. Ask questions. Find out what people are asking for that isn't being sold and you will see a market opening up. You can supply that empty need.

And since you did the research and asked the questions, you should have a list of names of the people who want that particular item.

Be creative and attend the local farmers market. Expand your horizons and visit *all* the farmers markets you can get to in a given time line. This will help you learn the ropes.

Most farmers markets have low cost spots available for you to sell your products. You can learn about production from listening to others talk about their items, learn lots about marketing, and you will look around and see what is selling well and what items are always left on the truck when the day is done.

Hobbies as Money Makers

Do you crochet, cross-stitch, quilt, build bird houses, whittle wood, create stepping stones, put together homemade candles, make pine needle baskets or design awesome homemade cards?

If you have a talent you can turn it into a money maker for country use! Yes, you can. Think outside the selling box. Take your projects to town and ask the store owners if you can set them in their stores on consignment. If the products sell well the owner may start buying the projects from you directly to resell in their store.

What sort of hobbies or talents do you have that you can turn into money makers? Do you collect things that you could make instead to create an income?

Of course you can announce all of these things for sale in your community newsletter and farm catalog!

"The wise man knows what he says, the foolish man says all he knows."

-Unknown

Sell Vegetables at the Farmers Market

Did you practice growing vegetables on your patio in the city? Want to grow a garden of real size and quantity now? Okay, lets get started!

Decide what will grow well in your area, keep the climate in mind when buying seeds. We can't grow corn or melons where we live because the growing season is too short. Instead we concentrate on root crops; onions, beets and potatoes.

Once you have your plot planned and planted you can check out your local or the closest, farmers market. This is where you take your produce to sell on a weekly or biweekly basis. Whatever you do, always take only the best quality and soon you will earn a reputation and get repeat buyers.

Farm Fresh Eggs

Raising chickens is the easiest for the start up farmer. In the spring, visit the local feed store and buy day-old chickens. Call to find out when they actually sell them, the time of year is different all over the world.

The book *"Farm Animals, Your Guide to Raising Livestock"* explains how to care for day-old chickens and adult chickens. Get a good book and refer to it for planning stages of raising any animal you choose. The above mentioned book gives the basics for all small farm animals including chickens, ducks, goats, pigs and cows.

Selling farm fresh eggs might not pay the mortgage but can be a very lucrative side business. If you start small and expand out as the business grows you will do very well. Start with a dozen hens and make sure you can sell or eat all the eggs. If that's no problem then buy another dozen and do the same. Soon you will have a lot of chickens and can be making a good sum of money each week.

How much can you charge for a dozen eggs? As of today we charge $2 a dozen and the buyers return the egg cartons when they come back for more.

Sometimes I give away a dozen eggs to new people. I do this as a marketing ploy. I know they will want to come back and buy more eggs after tasting the difference from the store bought ones they've eaten in the past. Store bought eggs are frozen for up to a year before they sell them to you.

"We cannot do everything at once but we can do something at once."

-Calvin Coolidge

Roadside Farm Stand

I've asked you before if you have a hobby or a talent that you could create as a money maker. A roadside farm stand would give you the opportunity to sell these items as well as veggies and fruits.

For starters, do you have chickens? Want to sell fresh eggs? A roadside stand would make it easy and convenient for folks to stop off on the way to or from work and pick up eggs.

> *"Just the thought or plan to go to town on Saturday was the source of great joy and anticipation.*
>
> *-Roy Webster*

Do you know how to make special coffees? You could sell those from your roadside stand during the morning rush hour and make a nice profit. I write books so I would sell farm books at my stand. I would also hand out a farm catalog to every customer and ask them to spread the word about our Farm Stand to their friends and families.

Give discounts if folks buy in bulk, such as buy four dozen eggs and get the 5th dozen free (when you have extra eggs to sell).

Everyone knows what great deals you can give and get when you have a small garden and sell fresh produce to folks. If you only sell quality products you will have enough return customers to keep your farm stand running all year round (depending on your climate, of course).

Farm Catalog

Creating a farm catalog to let others know about your services and products for sale makes perfect sense to me. You can keep it short and simple with a one-pager listing the product, what it will do for the buyer or a special feature such as 'organically grown', the price and your contact information so they can call to give you their order later.

Giving these farm catalogs away at feed stores, local grocery stores, the farmers market and any other place that will allow them, will get the word out and start your business booming.

Start a Community Newsletter

Once you're settled into your new home in the country and have some extra time, you can start a community newsletter. I would go around to businesses and ask if they would like to advertise in your newsletter; this could help pay for the print costs.

Why go to all of this trouble for the community? Well, you can announce sales within the area, you can let other farmers know when there will be a farm sale being held, you can also make sure every person who reads or looks at this newsletter knows what your own farm has to offer.

This could be a way to make income for the homestead selling fresh eggs, goat cheese or milk, piglets, fresh baked bread, etc.

Baking Bread

Another home based business can be baking bread for folks. Who doesn't love the smell of fresh bread? I love it! They even sell candles with this scent!

 Decide what you wish to bake every day... then create a catalog with product description and name. This can be a one or two page piece of paper. Keep it simple. You can add some tasty graphics to make it cute.

Now pass this out at the church, in convenience stores, grocery stores have free things in the entrance and you can put a stack there, stick one up in the laundrymat and outside the grocery store, on any bulletin boards you see in your town, etc. Get the word out.

Now you have to bake. If you created a nice catalog, put it up where a lot of folks can see it and made sure the correct contact information was there, they will call you. Wait until you get an order before you start baking!

Note about Humane Animal Husbandry

I have an inhumane story to tell you about every possible animal you can raise on a farm. I've been there. I've seen it all. But I don't want to waste paper telling you what I hope you already know.

I will give you one example before I start encouraging you to raise small farm animals for extra income. Imagine walking on to a farm to buy an animal. Lets say a piglet. As you walk up to the house which has the piglets you want to view, you see dead animals laying just off the walkway. Little babies like the one you were hoping to purchase.

When you enter the housing building for the piglets you see a huge mess. The smell has you holding your nose. Your eyes are watering from the sadness you see. What do you say to the seller?

All the pens are small but holding massive amounts of piglets. Some pigs are bigger than others and are jumping on the smaller ones' backs to get to the front of the row for your attention. They are probably praying you pick them and take them home.

The pens are completely full of mud and muck, probably tons of feces as well -since there isn't any other place for the piglets to leave their droppings. You don't see a trough for food or any container holding water. They have nothing! There is no sun light entering the building for the piglets and they have no access to an outside yard. What do you do?

Leave the premises and don't return. Give everyone you know the story so they don't buy from those kind of folks. Believe me, animals should have the best set up possible. Happy animals produce quality animals and good meat. Don't buy from people who don't know how to raise their animals humanely!

Remember this story when you are setting up pens for animals you raise for the dinner table. Just because you will eat them in the end doesn't mean that they don't deserve the best while they are in your yard. Be considerate and caring for animals.

Weaner Piglets

Raising weaner piglets is a huge business. I would advise to start small (as I always advise to do!) Buy one female and raise her up to breed. She will have anywhere from 8-15 piglets her first litter.

There is a big need for pork and people like the fresh taste much more than store bought. Actually, if we run out of sausage we can't stand to buy more from the store; we go without. It just doesn't taste good to us after having it fresh.

> *"Few animals and indeed few people are quite as shrewd or gifted with such a remarkable natural instinct as a sow."*
>
> -Louis Bromfield

What can you sell a piglet for? We sell our 6-week-old piglets for $65 each. Costs can vary depending on the time of year and equipment you need to raise them. We breed our sows so they're having piglets later in winter to sell early spring piglets for the fairs. So we need to use heat lamps and electric waterers which raise our costs. But we find it pans out just fine.

Pig Meat for Profit

Here's where you can make some extra money and get your freezer filled with pork for free.

Raise up four weaner piglets to butcher weight. 250 pounds is the average weight; over that weight it usually costs more per pound to put the weight on and it's more likely to be fat, not meat.

With four pigs it will cost about $50 a pig to raise them to butcher weight. If you have access to fruit from orchards or grow your own corn, etc, your costs will be a lot less. Otherwise I suggest buying in bulk or mixing your own. Remember if you have a milk goat you can add some milk to each feeding and save on some grain costs.

Once the pigs are raised to butcher weight, you can find buyers and sell three of the pigs to them. Now you keep the last pig for your own freezer needs and you will more than likely have enough money left over to buy another set of pigs to start the process over!

Raise and Sell Kids

I'm talking about goats here! Goats are awesome. You can do a lot with them. Kids are fun to have around. If you buy the milking breed you can

Four Good Reasons to Start a Country Business

Keep in mind that I run my own business from home and so it seems like the perfect place to work. Here are four reasons why you should start your own business. These are the advantages of having your own home-based office compared to working at a job.

1. You can move to the country anytime you want.

2. You can start or plan your business before you move if it's not strictly a local business.

3. Most rural jobs that you'll find right away are likely to pay less than a living wage in the city.

4. For you to find a job that's comparable to the well paid job you had in the city is difficult.

keep one for milk needs. Did you know
you can raise piglets on goat milk? It is
very high in nutrients and piglets thrive
on it. You can even milk your goat once
a day, instead of two or three. Just start
the milking schedule and stick to it from
the beginning.

Now think of what you can do with milk these days.
Cheese! Butter! Bread! Yogurt! Ice Cream! I make goat
cheese in all forms and love it. Folks buy it faster than
I can make it too.

You can use the whey from making cheese to make
homemade bread and it's wonderful. And you can use
the cheese to make a tasty pound cake. Just writing it
makes my mouth water.

"The highest compliment a New England man
could give a New England woman: 'Thar's one
thing I'll say for thet wife of yourn, my hawgs
ain't hed a square meal sence she come on the
premises."
— Bertha Damon, 1943

Beef to Pay Land Taxes

I like raising a cow for our freezer needs. But a cow would like some company and we can't use more than half a cow for our families table needs in one year. Here's what we do. We buy two calves in early spring. They keep each other company and protect one another from coyotes or other mishaps around here. By the following fall they are both ready to butcher and we find a buyer for one-and-a-half-cows.

We put half a cow into our freezer and get enough meat for the entire next year. Then we use the money from selling the other one-and-a-half cows to pay our land taxes and buy two more calves to start over the following spring!

Petting Zoo for Schools & Tours

This is a new idea for me. I want to start a petting zoo if I ever live close enough for folks to visit us. I figure if a person lived on a farm and it was near a large city they could do pretty good with a petting zoo.

Here's my idea. Figure out which animals you want to have. I thought a zoo with miniature animals would do real well. First build all the pens and buildings you would need for the animals. Then buy the animals and get used to them. See what it takes to raise them and learn the ropes of owning a zoo.

Next create a brochure to send to all the schools within a 50 mile radius of your farm. Make sure the brochure lists the prices and rules of your zoo. Such as children paying $5 a piece to attend, maybe having a discount for groups, bringing a brown bag lunch (you provide picnic tables), no smoking, etc.

When the bus arrives you welcome them all and give a tour of the zoo telling about each animal and its needs to survive. Then let the kids pet the animals and share in the hands-on education of the farm.

You make a nice chunk of dough for two hours work; the kids learn about animals and everyone is happy!

Small Dogs

Raising small dogs in the country can also be profitable. Do some market research to make sure there are buyers who are interested in the breed of dog you wish to raise before you invest. Otherwise you might end up with a lot of puppies you can't sell.

I would also recommend setting up the kennel first, before buying the dogs. This way you can overcome any obstacles before having the dogs to care for, too.

"A city is the physical manisfestation of an invisible reality, the souls of its people."
-John Osman, 1957

Building Log Furniture

I know someone who makes a living for a family of four building log furniture during the winter months. He's a carpenter for the rest of the year, so winter months are slow and he does very well building log furniture. If this attracts your attention, find books on the subject and learn to build log furniture in your spare time.

What type of wood is best for building log furniture? Black cherry and black walnut are a medium weight, strong and hard. These are both recommended for building log furniture.

Carving sticks

Can you carve small logs or sticks into beautiful shapes? This could be a great money maker. You can sell these objects you create at the farmers market.

Grow an Orchard

Are you good at growing fruit trees? If you are, then it might be profitable to grow your own orchard of fruit trees, pick what you wish to keep for canning and then let folks come in and pick what they want. Charge them by the box picked. They do the work; you get the money.

Another idea would be to grow an awesome strawberry or raspberry field and let folks do the same as above. They come and pick what they want and you charge them by the amount they pick.

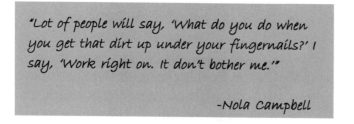

"Lot of people will say, 'What do you do when you get that dirt up under your fingernails?' I say, 'Work right on. It don't bother me.'"

-Nola Campbell

Cabin Rental for Different Seasons

If you have an unused cabin on your property, or can build one, it can bring you a bit of extra income. Even if you use it part time you can rent it out the other seasons of the year.

Maybe you don't use the cabin in the winter months? Rent it out to snowmobile renters and skiers. In the summer you can rent to campers and city folks who are trying to taste the country for a weekend.

Pond Rental

If you have a pond or lake on your property you can stock it with fish and charge fishermen and campers for the ability to fish in your pond.

Campgrounds

Personally the campground would have to be pretty far away from my house for me to agree to this adventure. I just don't want people camping in my yard.

But if you had enough acreage and could set up a nice campground area for folks to visit, I'm sure you could do quite nicely during the summer months. City folks love to get away from the every day chaos and forget about work for a weekend.

And if you set it up correctly you wouldn't have to be around all the time to baby-sit your customers. They would come, set up their tents or trailers, collect their firewood or twigs for starter wood, set up camp and get ready for the evening and you would sit back and collect the money!

Trailer Park

Of course this requires an investment on your part but not much work once it is set up. The trick would be to set the place up so that there is as little mainte-nance as possible for you to keep the place in shape.

Again, you can offer this seasonally to city folks who want to get away from work for a weekend. Or you might get full-time renters for your trailer park.

Bed & Breakfast

I would love to own a bed and breakfast and entertain different people all year long. I think it would be great to meet new people, learn about their discoveries in life and cook gourmet meals for them for a weekend or a night.

Again, if set up correctly there could be as little for you to worry about as possible. I once stayed at a bed and breakfast that offered old fashioned rooms. The an-tiques made you feel like you were back in the olden days visiting your past. The owners made themselves your friends right from the beginning. You were com-fortable the moment you walked in the door.

In the evening we were set at the old fashioned table in the dining room and the owners made us a gourmet dinner that I still haven't forgotten. In between cooking our meal they took the time to talk to us and we learned that the husband had built the entire building with his own hands. This was an eight room bed and breakfast! I was impressed.

General Store

If you live close to the road then maybe a general store is a consideration. Especially if there isn't one close by where you live. This way when folks are returning home and they forgot to pick up something they won't turn around and head back to town, they will come and visit you since your store will then be more convenient.

Save Yarn and Fabric Scraps

Even if you don't quilt or crochet, you can save extra yarn or fabric you come across for pennies at yard sales. Later when you have the time you can put these together to make things for Christmas or other holidays and birthday presents.

Or you can trade your own talents for the use of someone else's talents. Don't know what I mean? Do you know how to sew clothes or something? Want a blanket crocheted but don't know how to crochet?

You can save the scraps of fabric and/or the yarn and ask someone who does know how to crochet to make you a blanket. Then, you sew something for them.

"I could weave a yard a day, of the fine thread... Kept my foot a goin', and a throwin' that old-fashioned shuttle all day long."

-Clemmie Pugh, A People and Their Quilts

Keep Signs at the End of Your Driveway

Here is a great way to let drive-by's know of your products and services. I've seen some really great signs at the end of driveways in the country. You can have a chain linking all the different products you offer.

My favorite sign set up is a solid wood frame in the shape of the number 7. Along the downward stretch of the 7 shape, hanging downward from the top on a chain, you hang signs with each product or service you wish folks to stop in and buy.

The sign I am talking about had six wood sign links chained together. Each sign had a name of items they had for sale. Eggs. Dogs. Pigs. Rentals. Produce. You can even list each produce you offer such as onions, beets, tomatoes, corn, beans, etc.

Signs can be a very useful tool. If you are out of a product, you simply remove that sign from the post until it is back in stock.

Country Superstitions

♥   For good luck, sweep something into the house with a new broom, before you sweep something out.

♥   It is bad luck to take an old broom to a new house.

♥   Never buy a broom in May, for it sweeps all luck away.

♥   It is bad luck to turn a strange cat away from the door.

♥   It is bad luck to make a new opening in an old house.

♥   Leave a house by the same door through which you entered or you will be unlucky.

♥   If you rock the cradle empty, then you shall have babies plenty.

♥   If your apron falls from your waist, a new baby is on the way.

♥   A pregnant woman should only look on beautiful things so that her child should likewise be born well-favored.

♥ Newborns should be given three gifts; an egg to ensure plenty; silver to bring wealth; and salt for protection against enchantment.

♥ If a baby is put in the first April shower, it will always be healthy.

♥ A baby should be carried upstairs before downstairs so that it will rise in the world.

♥ To change a baby's name after you have named it will cause it to have bad luck all of its life.

♥ Holly was hung on the door at Christmas so that witches would stay outside counting berries.

♥ A horseshoe hung over the door, right way up to keep in the goodness, will keep witches away.

♥ Horse brasses hung over the fireplace are also a protection against witches.

♥ Wood spitting in the fireplace was believed to be the Devil coming down the chimney.

♥ Sneezing at the table is a sign of company at the next meal. If you sneeze while something is being said it is the truth.

♥ If you dream of a river, it means that something stands between you and your wishes.

♥ To dream of snakes brings bad luck.

♥ If you eat black-eyed peas on New Year's Day, you will have good luck all the year.

♥ A man must be the first person to cross your threshold on New Year's Day, or you will have bad luck throughout the coming year.

♥ When starting a journey, throw salt over your right shoulder to ensure safety.

♥ If you catch a falling leaf, you will have twelve months of happiness.

♥ To find a rusty nail is good luck. The nail should not be picked up, but the ends should be reversed, so luck will come your way.

♥ Stems of tea floating in the cup indicate strangers. The time of their arrival is determined by placing the stem on the back of one hand and smacking it with the other; the number of blows given before it is removed indicate the number of days before the stranger's arrival.

♥ It is unlucky to eat a fish from the head downwards; secure good luck by eating the fish from the tail towards the head.

♥ If a married man dreams that he is being married, it means that he is going to die.

♥ If you bring an axe or hoe or spade into the house on your shoulder, a member of the family will die soon.

♥ If a person dreams that he sees a naked figure dancing in the air, it means that death will come and release a soul from its body.

♥ If rain falls on a coffin, it indicates that the soul of the departed has "arrived safe."

♥ Never carry a corpse to church by a new road.

♥ If a cock crows at midnight, the angel of death is passing over the house.

♥ The howling of a dog is a sad sign. If repeated for three nights, the house will soon be in mourning.

♥ After a person dies, cover all the mirrors in the house to prevent the soul being caught.

♥ Hag stones -- flints with holes in them -- were at one time thought to be a safe guard against witches or evil, and were hung on stables and barns and under eaves of houses, or even carried in the pocket. And, if tied to the head of the bed, they would prevent nightmares.

♥ Rocks, of natural formation, with an opening or hole through which a person could crawl were thought to promote cures for backache, rheumatism and other ills.

♥ Jump across the doorsill when entering the house at night, so the spook cannot get hold of the heel left behind the other.

About the Author

Jeanie Peck moved from the big city ten years ago and has been farming on a small scale ever since. She lives with her family in Selah, Washington.

Jeanie created and publishes a 12-16 page quarterly newsletter about farming and raising farm animals. She loves to hear from folks who are just starting out and need advice, or who have been farmers for years and wish to share a story with her. You can get a sample issue for free by mentioning this book and writing to her at: PO Box 10445, Yakima, WA 98909, or by email at: info@OnTheFarmPress.com.

Jeanie has written two other books about farming; *Farm Animals, Your Guide to Raising Livestock* and *Pigs and other Stories*. You can find them in your local library, at your favorite bookstore or online at: www.OnTheFarmPress.com or visit Amazon.com today!

Appendix A

Rural Real Estate Checklist

Zoning, Building Codes & CC&R's

- Is the property in copliance with zoning and setback regulations?
- Are there any health, safety, or building code violations?
- If this is your plan, can you operate a homebased business in this property?
- Are there any notices of abatement or citations against the property other than the mortgage?
- Read CC&R's if any. Are there any violations apparent?

Parcel

- Is the property in a flood plain or special study zone?
- Is there any indication or does the owner know of any drainage problem?
- Is there any indication in the basement or on the property?
- Has the property been surveyed? Are the corners identified?
- If there is a stream, river or lake, does the property line run to the center?
- Are there any legal limitations on the use of any stream, river, ditch or lake property?

Road/Rights-of-way

- Is there a deeded Right-of-Way to the property?
- Is the road to the property public or private? Who maintains it? Snow removal?

Construction

- Are there any structural or foundation problems?
- Does the property have any urea-formaldehyde or asbestos material used in its construction?
- What type of roof? Age of roof? Any apparent leaking? Has attic been checked?
- Has the property suffered damage from a fire or a flood?
- What is the construction? Is it functional now?
- How long until it needs repair or replacement?
- What will it cost to repair or replace?
- What will it cost to maintain or operate?
- Can we live with it/without it?

Systems/Appliances

Are the following items in working order?

- Fan
- Doorbell
- Range
- Air Conditioning
- Sprinklers
- Microwave/Oven
- Garbage disposal
- Garage door opener

- Furnace
- Dishwasher
- Water softener
- Water pump/Sump pump
- Any problems affecting the plumbing, electrical heating or cooling, or the water heater?
- What were the owner's heating and air conditioning costs for the past 12 months?
- Is the sewage system public? If not, is there a septic system? Are there any blockages or breaks in the lines?
- Is there a septic system, is the owner aware of any backup or overflowing of the tank?
- Do any problems exist with permits, operation or system location?
- What was the date the septic system was last pumped?
- Where is it located?
- If the public sewage system is not hooked up what would the cost be to hook it up?
- If there isn't a septic tank in what would the total cost for a system be for your family size?

Water Source
- Is the water source public? Who is the water company? Approximate monthly cost for water?
- If the water isn't in, what would the cost be to hook it up?
- If the water source is public, is there any problem with the main line?

- Is there a well? Public or private? Is there a maintenance agreement between all parties?
- How deep is the well? What are the gallons per minute? Size of casing? What size horsepower is the pump on the well?
- Any problems with the water pressure or has the well ever run dry?
- Is there any contamination or other reason the water would not be potable?
- Is there irrigation water? What is the source? The cost?

Power
- Is there power to the property? If not, how far is the property from power?
- What would the cost be to bring power to the property?

Services
- Schools: What type? How far away? Is there bus pickup?
- Fire protection: How far away is the fire station?
- Medical care: What is the distance to nearest hospital? What about emergency treatment?
- Is there mail delivery? If not, how do you get your mail?

Legal

- Is there a Home Owners Association? If so, what are the dues per year?
- Are there any disputes with neighbors regarding location or use of driveways, patios, fences, common walls, etc.?
- Any condition or situation which might result in an increase in assessment?

The above was written with permission from the book, Discover The Good Life in Rural America by Bob Bone.

Appendix B

Change of Address Reminders

You'll need to put in a change of address as soon as possible for your new location so you don't miss any important incoming mail offers, and so your bills aren't late. Here are a few recommendations:

Family and Friends	IRS/other Tax Businesses
Drivers License	Car Registration
Voter Registration	Magazines
Life Insurance	Auto Insurance
Home Owners Ins.	Investments
Stock Broker	Car Loan
Bank	Airline Miles
Organizations	Clubs/Associations

Recommended Reading

Let us help in your search for the simple life. All the following items are available from us by mail order. Perfect for anyone with a country spirit, these tools will guide you toward comfortable, profitable living and make your relocation easier and more rewarding. Any of the following recommended reading can be ordered through the address below.

Communication Creativity
PO Box 909, Buena Vista, CO 81211-0909 US
Tel: 719-395-8659   Fax: 719-395-8374
E-mail: cc@SPANnet.org
Toll Free Order Line: 800-331-8355
www.CommunicationCreativity.com

Country Bound! Trade Your Business Suit Blues for Blue Jean Dreams by Marilyn and Tom Ross, Communication Creativity. A business book as well as a lifestyle guide, it addresses how to make a good living in Small Town USA. Marilyn and Tom Ross, who know from first hand experience, include hundreds of practical, thought-provoking ideas for prospering in paradise. You'll discover ways to turn spare-time interests into paying profits, telecommunicate to your present job, set up an Information Age home-based business, buy an existing rural enterprise, use the internet to access a global customer base, or create your dream job in the country. Dozens of quizzes, tables, checklists, maps and web sites to make your rural relocation easy, fun and economical. $19.95.

Discover The Good Life in Rural America
A City Slicker's Guide to Buying Country Real Estate Without Losing Your Shirt by Bob Bone, Communication Creativity. Hoping to buy real estate in Small Town USA? Here's a wish book to save you time, trouble and money! Whether your getaway place is a permanent family residence, a vacation retreat, a ranch or farm, a retirement home or investment property, this book points the way. Real estate expert Bob Bone provides you with sound advice for purchasing a piece of paradise. Handy checklists, tables of statistics and useful resources replace the worry and risk of buying country property with knowledge and confidence. $19.95.

Big Ideas for Small Service Businesses
How to Successfully Advertise, Publicize and Maximize Your Business or Professional Practice by Marilyn and Tom Ross. 224 pages. Loaded with idea generators, sample sales letters and checklists, this hands-on marketing manual saves you valuable time and expensive agency fees. It concludes with a resource section worth its weight in gold. Government sources, entrepreneurial contacts, and lists of suppliers provide specific guidance to help boost your profits. This book is chock-full of lessons about the very soul of the marketing process. A unique contribution to business marketing literature.

More Resourceful Books to Read...

To obtain any of the following books just visit your local library, your favorite book store, or Amazon.com. I suggest ordering them through your library first and buying only the ones that you wish to keep for reference books.

Working From Home: Everything you Need to Know About Living and Working Under the Same Roof, by Paul and Sarah Edwards, Jeremy Tarcher, Inc. The Edwards again team up here to offer their perceptive business advice. You'll learn about solving zoning problems, juggling family, friends, children and work, managing self-discipline and combatting the isolation factor. Loaded with useful nuts and bolts tips. $14.95.

Farm Animals: Your Guide to Raising Livestock 312 pages, www.On The Farm Press.com. Learn the basics for starting a small farm business with small farm animals. The daily chores defined. ISBN: 0-9716174-0-6. $18.95

500 More Things To Make For Farm and Home by Glen Charles Cook

Forest Farming by Sholto J. Douglas

Managing in a Time of Great Change by Peter F. Drucker

The Insiders Guide to Relocation
by Beverly Roman

Sell What You Sow
by Eric Gibson

Guerrilla Marketing Attack
Jay Conrad Levinson

Down on the farm
Stewart Hall Holbrook

Small Town Bound
John Clayton

Country Kids
Julie Kendrick

Continuing the Good Life
Helen Nearing

The Making of a Homesteader
Scott Nearing

Pastured Poultry Profits
Salad Bar Beef
both by Joel Salatin

Smart Money Guide to Bargain Homes
by James I. Wiedemer

The Contrary Farmer
Successful Berry Growing
At Nature's Pace
All three by Gene Logsdon

Country Wisdom
by David Larkin

Moving to the Country Once and For All
by Lisa Rogak

How to make $25,000 farming 25 acres
by Booker T. Whatley

You can order any of the following books from Storey Publishing through the following address:

Storey Publishing Books
Storey Communications, Inc.
RR1 Box 105
Schoolhouse Road
Pownal, Vermont 05261
http://www.storeybooks.com

Storey's Guide to Raising Pigs $18.95
Storey's Guide to Raising Rabbits $18.95
Storey's Guide to Raising Poultry $18.95
Storey's Guide to Raising Dairy Goats $18.95
Storey's Guide to Raising Beef Cattle $18.95
Keeping Livestock Healthy $19.95

Magazines

Countryside Small Stock Journal
W11564 Highway 64
Withee, WI 54498
(715) 785-7979

Small Farm Today
3903 West Ridge Trail Road
Clark, MO 65243
(800) 633-2535
Fax: (573) 687-3148

Mother Earth News
Ogden Publications
1503 SW 42nd Street
Topeka, KS 66609
(303) 682-2438

Acres USA
PO Box 8800
Metairie, LA 70011
(504) 889-2100

Stockman Grass Farmer
5135 Galaxie Drive, Suite 300C
Jackson, MS 39206
(800) 748-9808

Newsletters

I'm not kidding when I tell you there are a zillion places you can look for more help in your adventures. Try sending for a free or low cost sample of each of these newsletters and after browsing them real closely decide which ones will be right for you and subscribe.

Are you searching for RURAL PROPERTY?

You'll find it in this 52-page monthly magazine packed with rural and small town bargains — for sale by owners and agents NATIONWIDE!

**Farms · Ranches · Acreage · Recreation Property
Timberland · Waterfront · Rural Homes & Businesses**

Subscribe Today: $28/yr. (1st class) or $16/yr. (bulk mail) Sample: $3

Rural Property Bulletin

P.O. Box 369-F · Bassett, NE 68714

1-888-FARM-BUY (327-6289)

www.RuralProperty.net

Home Dairy News

The Home Dairy News, published 10x a year, is for homesteaders, home cheesemakers and wannabes interested in learning to produce dairy foods at home. Whether from fresh or purchased milk, you can experience the satisfaction that comes with producing your own yogurt, kefir, cultured butter, even Brie! HDN also features articles on the care and feeding of dairy animals - practical information you can use! Subscription $20/year. Send check or money order to Home Dairy News, P O Box 186-JP, Willis VA 24380. To order by credit card phone or fax (540) 789-7877 (24 hours). Print sample $1, or visit www.smalldairy.com.

On The Farm Newsletter
Of course this one I recommend everyone get a subscription for their Christmas buying gifts to family and friends and even folks you work with will enjoy the jokes, facts and fun humor of learning to farm on a small scale. If you order in quantity subscriptions, write or email for discounts! info@OnTheFarmPress.com
$12 year, or $3 sample
On The Farm Press, Sub. Dept.
PO Box 10445, Yakima, WA 98909

Catalogues
Call and request a free catalog from each of the following companies and see what peaks your interests.

Chuck Wagon Outfitters
800-798-2359
Cast iron cookware and accessories.

Direct Line
800-241-2197
Power tools, generators, air tools and pumps.

Gemplers
800-382-8473
Outwear: Boots, rain gear, etc. Step ladders. Lots of stuff here for the country setting.

Hoegger
800-221-4628
Goat and cheesemaking supplies.

Jeffers

800-533-3377

Livestock medical and every day supplies, tools, tags, even electric fencing supplies.

Lehmans Non-Electric

330-857-5757

Everything you would need to live more self-sufficiently.

Lionel Industries

561-624-9093

Egg and poultry supplies.

Nasco

800-558-9595

All country needs including livestock supplies, scales, boots, traps, equipment for livestock.

Tek Supply

800-835-7877

Floodlights, overhead doors, alarms, fans, timers.

On The Farm Press

Email: info@OnTheFarmPress.com

Farm books, useful booklets, newsletter.

Helpful Websites

The vast web still amazes us all. If you want to use the web to obtain more information you will be surprised at just how much you can find. Here are a few websites that are available for agriculture adventures. Use your search engines to look up even more data!

Tips for buying rural property -book
http://www.govbiz.com/buyingtips.htm

Free Relocation Package
Select state and city to receive your free gift
http://www.erelocationprofessionals.com

Country Bound -book
http://www.Communication Creativity.com

Homesteading and Small Farm Resources
http://www.homestead.org

Foreclosed HUD or For-Sale-by-Owner Homes
http://www.bargain.com

Cooperative Extension Services
http://www.reeusda.gov

Corporate Relocation
RelocationCentral by CORT arranges housing and furniture nationwide. http://www.relocationcentral.com

Moving and Relocation Help
Free online estimate request form. Find moving tips, guides and more.
http://www.LocalMoverDirectory.com

Index

A

B

C

F

G

H

I

ice 136
instant pantry 121
internet 65

J

jobs in the country 144

K

keeping dogs 127
kids. *See* Moving
knives 136

L

leather 136
living expenses 32
log furniture 162

M

medical 35
mineral rights 82
money makers 149

N

natural hazards 83
neighbors 93
number of acres 72

O

odor 137
off the grid 110
offer services 41
orchard 163

Farm Animals;
Your Guide to
Raising Livestock

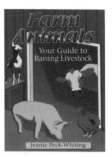

2003, 312 pp.
6 x 9, $18.95
ISBN# 0-9716174-0-6
How to raise small farm animals.
Compared to 'All Creatures Great & Small'

QN-300
On-The-Farm
Quarterly Newsletter
$12 year, $3 Sample Issue
Awesome Farm Newsletter helps
promote small-farmers across America
through real life experiences. Our *On-The-Farm Newsletter* has **subscribers
in 24 states. Ask your librarian to
subscribe for you!**

Booklet #300
Farrowing 101:
Short Guide to the
World of Farrowing

2002, 24 pages
5 x 8, Saddle Stitched
Free Pull-Out Poster
$5.95
From buying a female for breeding,
to raising the piglets, this booklet
has all the info you need to get started.

- One 500 pound pig will leave 11,860 pounds of manure in your yard every year!

- Did you know that ONE pig can drink 4 gallons of water a day?

- Captains once kept pigs on board because they thought pigs would swim towards shore after a ship wreck.

- Pigs are the number one livestock animal for meat production in the world.

- More than 5 billion cans of SPAM have been sold since 1937, when it was introduced.

- In 1884 Anthony Melton (a boy from Houston) was saved from drowning by a pig called Priscilla.

Booklet #225
Small-Farm Records

2002, 17 pages
8 x 11, Saddle Stitched
$7.95

17 pages with sample reports
charts, and ready-to-use sheets
for your convenience.

Annual Round-Up
Instruction Booklet

2002, 24 pages
5 x 8, Saddle Stitched
$5.95

Learn how to throw a party that
family & friends will talk about
for years! Have a BBQ, hayride,
egg toss, give away prizes, includes
a recipe to make 4 pans of lasagna.

Farrow to Finish
Video

2004
30 minutes
ISBN: 0-9716174-1-4
Category: Agriculture/Animals
$19.95

This 30 minute video shows it all.
See the sow in her own surroundings,
view the piglets being born in head and
feet first presentations, learn what to
take with you to the farrowing pen,
and how to raise up butcher weight
hogs.

Order Form

Qty	Title	Price	Total

Subtotal	
Shipping & Handling: $5.00 total order	
International Shipping add $10 for Global	
7.6% tax (WA residents only)	
Total	

Name _____ Date _____

Address _____

City _____ State _____ Zip _____

☐ Check Enclosed Bill My: ☐ Visa ☐ Mastercard

Card# _____

Exp.date _____ Signature _____

On The Farm Press
PO Box 10445, Yakima, WA 98909
(509)697-4014 Fax: (509)698-6425
Email: info@OnTheFarmPress.com